"*The Heart of the Fight* is an inspirational and eye-opening wake-up call for anyone who wants to create authentic, thriving relationships. From friendships to business relationships to spouses, this book provides great tools for relationships that really work. The book challenges the status quo and opens our eyes to a whole new way of looking at something."

> —**Jack Canfield**, coauthor of the *New York Times* #1 best-selling book series *Chicken Soup for the Soul*

"I have known the Wrights for years and have always been impressed by their grounded approach to relationship and life. They bring an unusual blend of practicality and integrity to their cutting-edge work that eschews simple answers. Their groundbreaking method and research should take its place as simply the most practical, effective approach to maximizing couple and individual potential and satisfaction."

> —**Barnet Bain**, film director of *Milton's Secret*, producer of *What Dreams May Come*, and author of *The Book of Doing and Being*

"*The Heart of the Fight* by Judith and Bob Wright is one of those books that is based on good social scientific evidence, the authors' own and others' research, and yet is written in a lively enough prose style that couples who need the advice will actually enjoy reading it."

> —**Barbara J. Risman, PhD**, fellow at the Center for Advanced Study in the Behavioral Sciences, professor of sociology at the University of Illinois at Chicago, vice-president of the American Sociological Association, president of the Southern Sociological Society, and president of the board of the Council on Contemporary Families

"Judith and Bob Wright draw upon thirty years of research into couples, relationships, and human behavior, as well as their own long marriage, to tell an eye- and heart-opening truth: the conflicts we think we should avoid in our relationships are exactly where we have to go in order to achieve the genuine connection, intimacy, and mutual growth we want in our relationships. This is the must-have manual for lasting and meaning-ful relationships."

> —**Patricia Crisafulli**, best-selling author, and founder of www .faithhopeandfiction.com

"At last, here's a brilliant manual for couples that really works. The secret: based on their extensive counseling of couples, Bob and Judith Wright explain why 'great relationships require great fights.' Don't stop fighting, but learn from the Wrights how to fight properly and creatively while you battle your way to bliss. ... If you feel your daily relationship is like going over Niagara Falls without a barrel, it's time to get to calmer waters by fighting hard while fighting clean. This book will show you how."

> —**Larry Kirshbaum**, former CEO of Time Warner Book Group, and literary agent

"The best relationships, from friends to dates to partners, are the ones where we are willing to deeply engage. The Wrights have put together a breakthrough guide that teaches how to develop the relationship muscles we all need by engaging rather than avoiding."

> —**Sonia Choquette**, *New York Times* best-selling author of *The Answer is Simple*

"I know the Wrights and have seen their work. I've spoken with their students and been impressed by the vitality, clarity, and forthrightness of their interactions. We have discussed their research and I am consistently impressed by the solidity of their approach and the fact that they practice what they preach. What they are saying in *The Heart of the Fight* is grounded in years of experience and success. Don't miss this opportunity to understand the basic elements and finer points of relationship success."

> —**Brad Anderson**, former CEO of Best Buy

"Lovers hate conflicts. Employees hate conflicts. Your pets hate conflicts. ... But conflicts—and the fighting that ensues—are unavoidable, and the more deeply you love someone, or want to love someone, the more fights you are going to have. ... But if you fight fairly, with love within your heart, your intimacy will prosper. Judith and Bob Wright will show you the 'right' and 'wrong' way to fight, making this a rare and valuable book for every couple and spouse."

> —**Mark Waldman**, executive MBA faculty at Loyola Marymount University, and coauthor of *How Enlightenment Changes Your Brain*

"*The Heart of the Fight* is the first book I've ever read and loved this much that gives couples practical advice for reframing conflicts in ways that strengthen their ability to stay married forever! I was mesmerized with their new terminology for conflict and with their universally appealing ways to unlock and sustain healthy neurochemistry—even through rocky challenges that might normally take couples down paths of no return when conflict and crisis emerge. Heading into my forty-sixth year of marriage, I found some new and beautiful suggestions for ensuring that the strength of healthy conversations with my husband prevails. This is a must-read book for all couples ready to get married, or in a marriage they want to keep for life!"

> —**Judith E. Glaser,** author of *Conversational Intelligence*; CEO of Benchmark Communications, Inc.; and chairman of The CreatingWE Institute

"I love this book! Bob and Judith offer the best program I've seen for using the conflict that inevitably arises in marriage to help a couple create more intimacy. This is a must-read for anyone in a relationship or thinking about getting in a relationship."

> —**Cynthia Kersey,** visionary and global humanitarian, founder and CEO of Unstoppable Foundation, and best-selling author of *Unstoppable*

"The Wrights are not afraid to get down and dirty, right smack into the middle of the messiness of relationship. They teach that only by learning from our fights can we unlock the key to real connection and intimacy. They made believers out of us!"

> —**Marc Malnati,** owner of Lou Malnati's Pizzeria; and **Jeanne L. Malnati, LCSW,** culture transformation expert

"*The Heart of the Fight* starts with a mind-bending premise: that the purpose of relationships is not to make you happy; it is to make you your best. ... Big thumbs-up for an unusual, powerful, insightful, and loving approach."

> —**Tony Simons, PhD,** associate professor at Cornell University, and author of *The Integrity Dividend*

"Aspiring to the ideal of a 'marriage made in heaven' sets us up for disappointment. Conflict is part of every relationship—business and personal—and learning to develop the capacity for constructive discontent is truly the key to long-term relational success. This is a breakthrough book about the power of using conflicts to get closer—really closer—not the fairy-tale version, but the strong, robust kind that comes with shared experience, getting to know each other more deeply, and developing enduring trust."

> —**Blaine Bartlett**, president and CEO of Avatar Resources, adjunct professor at Beijing University, and board member of the World Business Academy

"A unique and refreshing approach to embracing conflict in relationships, Bob and Judith practice what they teach—and boy, do they teach it with clarity. Brimming with new insights, [the book] is chock-full of grounded examples. It's a must-read! Don't miss the opportunity to take your relationship to another level."

> —**Ray Blanchard, PhD**, visionary leader, coproducer of *The ANSWER to Absolutely Everything*, and coauthor of the best seller *The Art and Science of Success*

"I've read a number of books about how to better love your spouse or partner, but I have not seen or read a book about how to 'fight' better. We know that there will be fights, so why not learn how to fight more fairly? That made a lot of sense to me. But Bob and Judith went beyond just the basics to deliver an exceptional set of strategies for fighting for the ultimate goal—a sustainable, thriving relationship. Thanks for this tool that I know will benefit both me and my husband for many years!"

> —**Melissa G. Wilson**, coauthor of *Networking is Dead*

"As a Jungian therapist who has worked with couples like Judith and Bob Wright write about in *The Heart of the Fight*, I found no hollow ring to any of their stories. Rather, they have laid out a game plan for couples to get out of the blame game and rediscover why they are together in the first place."

> —**Albert Clayton Gaulden**, founding director of The Sedona Intensive, and author of *You're Not Who You Think You Are*

"All couples experience conflict and get into fights. The critical element is to not let the fight get the better of the relationship. Based solidly on research and counseling experience, Bob and Judith Wright have written a remarkable guide to help couples manage conflict and to turn what could be a lose-lose situation into a win-win."

> —**Ronald E. Riggio, PhD**, Henry R. Kravis professor of
> leadership and organizational psychology at the Kravis
> Leadership Institute at Claremont McKenna College, and
> coauthor of *Transformational Leadership*

"Feel like fighting? Push pause for a bit and make sure you're doing it the Wright way! Bringing Bob in to work with our leadership team in person last year took their ideas about effective engagement, fighting fair, and engaging in constructive conversations into play within our organization. It's not always easy, but it's very rewarding. The Wrights' rules of engagement help us all to rise to the next level. Everything goes better when we master getting to the heart of the fight!"

> —**Ari Weinzweig**, author, and **Paul Saginaw**; co-owners and
> founding partners of Zingerman's Community of Businesses,
> and winners of the lifetime achievement award from *Bon Appétit*
> magazine

"If you could be a fly on the wall listening to other couples, you would hear the same fifteen triggers that start most fights. Paradoxically, these explosions unearth treasures which, when mined properly, serve to strengthen the relationship. Bob and Judith's book, based upon thirty years of experience in couples counseling, is essential reading for anyone in a relationship or hoping to be."

> —**David Mager**, co-COO of Deepak HomeBase, and friend from
> Social Venture Network

"Bob and Judith Wright have provided us with an amazing playbook for couples who want to experience the joy of authentic intimacy. *The Heart of the Fight* is a powerfully practical resource for transforming you and your couple."

> —**Rich Blue, MA, LCPC, NCC, BCPPC**, author of *Surprised by*
> *God*, and founder and clinical director of the Center for
> Christian Life Enrichment

"Judith and Bob Wright excel at connecting the dots between dreams and deliverables. Highly mutual and grounded in practicality, their tools and strategies have catalyzed key personal transformations in me that have been essential for growth and success in business and the world."

—**Matt Booty,** former president and CEO of Midway Games

the
heart
of fight
the

A Couple's Guide
to 15 Common Fights,
What They Really Mean &
How They Can Bring You Closer

JUDITH WRIGHT, EdD
BOB WRIGHT, EdD

New Harbinger Publications, Inc.

Publisher's Note

This publication is designed to provide accurate and authoritative information in regard to the subject matter covered. It is sold with the understanding that the publisher is not engaged in rendering psychological, financial, legal, or other professional services. If expert assistance or counseling is needed, the services of a competent professional should be sought.

Author's Note

The Heart of the Fight *is intended for functional couples to explore their potential, not to replace psychotherapy.*

Distributed in Canada by Raincoast Books

Copyright © 2016 by Judith Wright and Bob Wright
New Harbinger Publications, Inc.
5674 Shattuck Avenue
Oakland, CA 94609
www.newharbinger.com

Cover design by Amy Shoup; Interior design by Guido Caroti;
Acquired by Melissa Kirk; Edited by Gretel Hakanson

Library of Congress Cataloging-in-Publication Data

Names: Wright, Judith, 1951- | Wright, Bob, 1948-
  Title: The heart of the fight : a couple's guide to fifteen common fights,
    what they really mean, and how they can bring you closer / Judith Wright,
Bob Wright.
  Description: Oakland, CA : New Harbinger Publications, 2016. | Includes biblio-
graphical references.
  Identifiers: LCCN 2015030913| ISBN 9781626252578 (paperback) | ISBN
    9781626252585 (pdf e-book) | ISBN 9781626252592 (epub)
  Subjects: LCSH: Marriage. | Marriage counseling. | Conflict management. |
    BISAC: FAMILY & RELATIONSHIPS / Marriage. | FAMILY &
RELATIONSHIPS /
    Conflict Resolution. | PSYCHOLOGY / Psychotherapy / Couples & Family.
  Classification: LCC HQ503 .W75 2016 | DDC 306.81--dc23 LC record available at
http://lccn.loc.gov/2015030913

Printed in the United States of America

18   17   16

10   9   8   7   6   5   4   3   2

To the dedicated couples who have worked with us to develop this model, who bravely battle to bliss, get to the heart of the fight, and forge new paths of intimacy. They are an inspiration and incalculable blessing to our world.

Contents

Introduction 1

Part 1: Real Relationships: Breaking Myths and Building Vision

1 The Adventure of Intimate Conflict. 7

2 Love Is Messy 25

3 Happily Never After: Getting Past Fairy-Tale Romance
So You Can Fight for True Love.. 41

Part 2: The Art of the Fight: Six Skills for Battling to Bliss

4 Yearn: Discover and Follow Your Yearning 61

5 Engage! The Seven Rules for Fighting Fair and Loving Well 81

6 Reveal: Uncover the Matrix of Your Unconscious Beliefs and
Unfinished Business .. .. .103

7 Liberate: Break Free from Limiting Beliefs and Behaviors . .. .. .125

8 Rematrix: Reprogram Your Mind, Transform Your Relationship 145

9 Dedicate: Commit to Change for the Better, Forever .. .. .165

Part 3: Open Your Heart and Expand Your Vision

10 Emotional Maturity: Intimate Living, Loving, and Fighting. .. .. .183

11 Intimate Intelligence: The ABCs of Emotional Literacy. .. .. .193

12 The Good Fight: An Expanding Vision of What Is Possible. .. .. .209

Acknowledgments 221

References 223

About the Authors 231

Resources. 234

Introduction

We're going to share with you what we have learned about how to look deeply into the heart of the fight. Based on our research and work with couples along with proven psychological principles and current research in relationships and neuroscience, this book will facilitate your efforts to

- fight productively and use your fights to get closer, rather than farther apart;

- identify the deeper motivation behind your conflict;

- learn and grow to get more of what you desire;

- experience more deep love.

Prepare for an adventure in relating. We'll provide you with tools that will help you explore the potential of partnering—learning to live deeply ever after. We'll share a process to discover what's really going on between you and your partner—and within yourself—when you fight. This knowledge will guide you to go beyond fights into the adventure of learning, growing, and transforming together.

This book is an outgrowth of many years of working with couples at the Wright Graduate University and our Realization of Human Potential curriculum. In easy-to-understand language, it integrates the theory and research that underlie this curriculum, which includes the best of what we call human emergence technologies.

Mutuality is a key principle of our work. That means that we are learning and growing along with you. You will read a good deal about the two of us, warts and all—and how, in our relationship, we have applied and are applying the six bliss skills you will be learning. When you see a first-person story, it is one of us sharing.

Throughout, we'll refer to fifteen fights—conflict types that might sound different on the surface but have remarkable similarities. You will find that the content of any two fights can appear as different as a Maasai warrior and a Swedish doctor, but they operate on the same principles and reveal the same truths. It may seem as if a disagreement about who takes out the trash is nothing like a donnybrook involving jealous accusations, but when you look into the heart of the fights, you'll find common themes and dynamics.

Understand, too, that many of your beliefs about relationships and conflict may be based on myths and misconceptions. Get ready to question what you've been taught about relationships. In fact, start out with these myth-busting truths:

- Chemistry does not make great relationships.

- Finding the right person isn't the answer.

- Working on your relationship doesn't work—working on yourself does.

- Communication skills don't lead to great relationships and conflict resolution isn't the best way to deal with your fights.

- The purpose of a relationship isn't to make you happy; it's to make you your best.

Sound different? As we hope you'll agree, it also sounds like a much better and more realistic way to deal with relationships.

How to Use This Book

The Heart of the Fight has three parts: Part 1 sets the stage by exploding myths of relationships and recognizing the wealth of benefits available when we get to the heart of the fight. Part 2 takes you by the hand and introduces you to the six skills to get to the heart of the fight with plenty of tips and applications for you to experiment with as you learn the skills that not only resolve conflict but also generate rich experiences with plenty of nourishing intimacy. Part 3 gives you an opportunity to firm up and explore your new, emerging vision for your intimate relationship.

In each section, you'll find entertaining and informative stories of real-life couples we've worked with. You'll find advice about how to fight productively and how to avoid useless conflict. And you'll encounter fascinating studies and examples from neuroscience to existentialism to hit Broadway shows that provide insight into this advice.

You don't even need to be in a relationship to use this book, and you don't need to know any of the science. This book weaves the science into a straightforward process of six skills with plenty of exercises and experiments to help you explore and discover what works for you. You don't need to do the exercises now; you can always circle back and do them later. Above all, keep reading.

Much of what you will be learning is counterintuitive and even against common, everyday, so-called wisdom, but it is what works. That is why we look at and debunk everyday mythology. Getting to the heart of the fight requires that you identify your own myths and understand how they derail real, everyday, sleeves-rolled-up intimacy.

As you encounter the book's numerous exercises and tips, understand that, whether you do them or not, they are designed to operate as seeds for a rich vision of possibility that can grow in your unconscious mind as you engage in your life adventure. The six *battling to bliss* skills that take you to the heart of the fight provide a simple-to-understand structure to solidify your new insights.

It is the small moves that make the big differences. You will learn about the yearning at the heart of the fight and how to tap and follow it to new ways of interacting. Don't take our word for it. Experiment; make the bliss skills and discoveries your own.

This book is not about managing conflict, but embracing it for greater love and satisfaction. We're going to ask you to reexamine your relationship values, look into your motivations, accept some of your less-than-admirable qualities, and see the valid motivations beneath even the most embarrassing of your personal traits and messy, embarrassing fights.

Keep your sense of humor at the ready as you read; we have always appreciated the role of laughter and humor in self-acceptance—and in helping us get underneath the conflict. So get ready to laugh, be amazed, and even cry a little as you dig into relationship conflict, get to the heart of the fight, and discover the riches in the adventure of intimacy through conflict.

PART 1

Real Relationships

Breaking Myths and Building Vision

CHAPTER 1

The Adventure of Intimate Conflict

"Are you sure you don't want a divorce?" the marriage counselor asked me as Bob left the room for a restroom break from our double session.

I look at him askance, saying, "No. Why are you asking me that?"

"Because you are fighting, and it's so intense."

The counselor didn't understand getting to the heart of the fight. He thought that vehement arguments signified a bad relationship. He was also uncomfortable with our level of engagement, truth, and real feelings.

This was the second time that a marital counselor we had seen got hung up on the conflict and missed the larger adventure of authentic, genuine interaction and growth that we were on. Each of us knew that we were in this relationship to learn and grow and become our best selves—that we were always working on ourselves even when fighting to change each other's behaviors.

Bob had legitimate issues he was fighting for, but, like me, was far from wanting a divorce. We loved one another and relished the challenge of growing a real, truthful union. Our relationship was never seriously in question. We generally fought for outcomes, not to resist or punish each other. We sought counseling, not because we were "in trouble," but so we could resolve the conflict, gain insight into our patterns, and understand ourselves better.

Our fights certainly weren't (and still aren't) the sort of refined, enlightened debates you might imagine. They involved stomping around, yelling, frustrating exchanges, and silent withdrawals. But afterward, when we worked things out, they always led to more understanding of ourselves, empathy for each other, and closeness. Most of our fights are quick now, so quick, in fact that our staff complain that they never have time to get their cell phones out to record them (as examples of efficient conflict resolution). In the early days, I was the more defensive one, not wanting to look at my dark side or admit things like I really wasn't as nice as I wanted people to think I was. I really did want to hurt Bob at times. My unconscious wish to hurt him was a mistaken attempt to be understood—maybe if he felt like I did, he'd finally understand! I saw and continue to see how much of my past I project onto Bob—like my discovery that the understanding I craved from him was a long-standing need from my childhood and that my anger at his occasional distance is only partially due to him.

While Bob generally stays more responsible than I during our fights, he doesn't reveal his vulnerability or fear as much as his anger and hurt. Eventually, we cool off and move to responsible positions. At this point, we are often amazed at the information and personal learning that surface in fights and the intimacy we develop.

In the early years, we were discovering a whole new way of relating inspired by Bob's work in the human potential movement as well as Adlerian, developmental, and existential psychology. We had principles to follow, but no template. Fighting and expressing full-out was bringing us much more closeness, understanding, and intimacy than playing nice or being careful and restrained with our words.

And it wasn't just us. We have been doing relationship coaching and leading couples programs and groups for over thirty years, almost as long as we've been married. We've been blessed to work with hundreds of couples, not just those in trouble, but couples who want the most out of their relationships and their lives. We've seen couples throughout many phases of their relationship, so we know what works over the long haul. We have done coaching, training, couples starting with premarital work throughout all marriage to after their kids graduated from college.

We did a groundbreaking research study of those mate, thriving relationships and were blowing the door lives in all areas. We discovered that they followed a process that not only helped them get to the heart of their conflicts, but that same process also led to deep intimacy and fulfillment in all areas of their lives. As researchers and teachers, we're also able to put relationship conflict in a larger context. We have founded a nationally accredited graduate university offering master's and doctoral degrees where we train professional coaches and leaders, integrating the best of human emergence technologies and the latest behavioral and neuroscience research.

So we know what it really takes to have a thriving, intimate, loving relationship—and it's not what you think nor is it what we'd been taught through our training, much less from our families, folktales, media, popular movies, and books.

Great Relationships Require Great Fights: The Results Are Worth It

Do you want maximal warmth and affection? The price is being real. Does profound partnership appeal to you? Then learn to express your deepest truths. Interested in intimacy? Then intend to be satisfied. In short, do you want a great relationship as best friends and lovers? Then be prepared for great fights.

Unfortunately, most people (including many professionals) don't know how to fight—or don't fight enough, or at all! They tend to teach conflict resolution rather than conflict completion. Contrary to conventional wisdom, conflict can be a couple's secret weapon for coming closer, not a sign they're coming apart—at least when couples know why they fight, how to fight, and what to fight for.

These battles can be used to develop us and help us reach high levels of intimacy and trust based on an ever-deepening love. This requires full engagement, including conflict, confrontation, and verbal combat. It also requires following certain rules of engagement that you'll learn about throughout the book. Most people bicker and battle without knowing the rules of engagement that will help them really see what is going inside of themselves. They just want the fight to be over, or to win the fight, or to make it go away. Most relationship books and much marital and relationship advice are designed to limit conflict, full of misguided attempts to restore the lovey-dovey honeymoon phase. They attempt to avoid fights and at best to develop teamwork rather than embrace the opportunity for learning and growth in the fights.

The Fifteen Fights That Make or Break Your Relationship

To understand the right way to fight, think about fight types. By categorizing relationship battles, we can help put you in the middle of a recognizable conflict. You'll resonate immediately with certain fight types that characterize your relationship, and you'll be able to analyze your fighting style and substance within these familiar categories.

What follows is a quick overview of the fights. We picked the most frequent types we encounter to illustrate the opportunity to develop the skills you will be learning and to show you how they work in your conflicts and your relationships. You will find these relationship fight types sprinkled throughout the book. It is not the topic of the disagreement that matters. It's what the fight means to the two of you and what you can learn from it. While couples often argue about the same surface issues, the underlying issues are personal to the two of you—and it's the underlying issues that need to be dealt with, not the surface topic.

Take a look at these fifteen fight types and think about how they unfold within your relationship.

1. The Blame Game

Here the fight is over who is at fault—for a lousy vacation, a crummy restaurant choice, an obnoxious visitor overstaying her welcome, or the argument itself. There's a big difference between scapegoating and figuring out why something went wrong. The former is a vindictive activity while the latter is a learning exercise. Getting caught in the Blame Game often results in endless loops of dissatisfaction with no real change.

Instead of assigning blame in arguments, figure out what you're so upset about, what went wrong, and how to change it now and in the future. As you look underneath, you'll discover why it is that you are so concerned about affixing blame. Then you can focus instead on what it will take for you to be satisfied.

2. Up and Down Toilet Seats and Other Domestic Disputes

Petty squabbles such as disagreements about chores, toilet seats, and neglected and unappreciated *Cinder(f)ellas* cover a range of domestic disputes from who's washing the dishes, picking up the kids, making dinner, and doing the laundry to arguing over how chores should be done. These are often fights over the distribution of duties or minimizing and demeaning each other's domestic contributions.

There are power and control struggles at unconscious levels in all relationships that often play out in squabbles over who does what or how tasks should be done. If you bicker without resolution or one of you gives in to end the fighting, nothing is learned. Rather than drag the relationship down, these domestic duty duels can be opportunities for relationship growth. This skirmishing serves a purpose, helping to resolve or at least expose issues that would otherwise eat away at the fabric of the relationship.

3. Dueling Over Dollars

Financial feuds—whether about making money, spending it, using it the way you want, managing it (or not)—are volatile topics for many couples. These fights range from "Are you crazy? We can't afford that!"

to "You're such a tightwad!" Or, it may begin innocently enough, with one person saying out of concern, "Why don't you ask for a raise?" But concern can easily segue into anger when the response to the question fails to satisfy: "You're just not motivated to get ahead and make something of yourself."

Money—lack of it, making more of it, how it's spent or managed—may be a valid concern; however, money is only the surface subject of the argument. Money is powerfully symbolic of many diverse things depending on the individual. These fights often mask issues of self-worth, values, or a sense of security. They can stem from a desire to be appreciated, other unmet desires such as keeping up with the Joneses, or hunger for social affirmation. We all want to be loved, and we easily make the mistake of equating enough money with enough love. Evolutionary biology and neuroscience also show us that having enough resources is linked with survival in our primitive brains, so any threat of money scarcity can trigger our (often irrational) primal fear—and feisty fights.

4. The Hidden Middle Finger

You walk away, seething, silent, and resentful—now it's time for the silent treatment. "That ought to show him" is the message you're sending, but it rarely gets through. Nothing is resolved, and the relationship never deepens.

Relationship fights can be deadly quiet; you can say, "screw you," without raising your voice or even saying a word. In fact, Hidden Middle Finger fights often involve silence. You can simply pretend the disagreement isn't there. In fact, other exchanges can seem placid and even friendly on the surface. Beneath it, however, passive-aggressive behavior is eroding the relationship.

Getting the discussion to the point where actual upset and anger are expressed and the hidden middle finger is out in the open is critical. Some couples simply don't have much social-emotional intelligence. By developing their ability to express their feelings beyond their middle finger and interact more truthfully with each other, they grow in understanding, intimacy, and satisfaction.

5. Sexual Dissatisfaction

These arguments range from "You never are in the mood!" to "You're always in the mood," or "You're just going through the motions," or "You don't find me attractive anymore." These fights are about more than sexual intimacy, and they can be mined for valuable information about how to have better intercourse in all ways, making the relationship—as well as the sex—better. Looking at the host of issues beneath the intercourse will help avoid destructive arguing that can profoundly undermine the self-confidence of both parties.

Our research reveals that our adult sexual needs are often secondary to unmet developmental needs. While the power of adult sex can play a significant role in our development, we often have much younger, presexual needs to be affirmed, seen, known, and cared about. Getting to the submerged yearnings of each person deepens the level of intimacy and takes the conversation beyond the number of times you do it weekly, which tends to go up when couples argue productively together without necessarily focusing on it or keeping score.

6. If You Really Loved Me, You'd...

If you really loved me, you'd quit smoking, come home sooner, know what to buy me without me telling you, stop watching so much TV, spend less time with your computer games, refrain from buying so many shoes, dress better. There are infinite variations on this relationship fight: "If you really loved me, you'd take my side when your mother criticizes me," or "If you really loved me, you wouldn't speak that way to me."

Rather than getting sidetracked on the false premise that people in love should mind-read and provide unconditional obedience to wishes, the conversation should focus on understanding why you, or your partner, play the "if you really loved me" card. Great insights reside in these arguments about what love really means to each of you and what the responsibilities of love are. You each may have a different view, but facing these different perspectives square on can help you grapple with a major emotional roadblock and elevate the relationship.

7. I Can't Stand the Way You...

"I can't stand your constant harping." "Why do you have to treat the waitress that way?" "We're not in the backwoods here; smacking your lips like that is so rude." All of a sudden you can't stand the way your partner chews, walks, eats, or talks. Simple everyday habits bug you or even make your skin crawl. Things that were endearing in the past start grating on your nerves: "If he does that one more time, I'll scream" or "Every time she uses that tone of voice, it's like fingernails on a blackboard."

Almost anything can become irritating or begin to annoy or aggravate you. Look beneath these "you bug me" type fights, and you'll start to find a lot of unexpressed upsets that have been swept under the carpet—and now you're tripping on it. A loud laugh, the sound of cracking knuckles, a certain facial expression, or a once-endearing nervous tic is now sending you through the roof. Something is bugging you, but it's not what you think. You need to recognize the deeper issues so you can move the relationship forward.

8. You Love _____ More than Me

"You love your iPhone/sports/shopping/Facebook/work/the kids… more than me" is the theme of these battles. It may come out as a direct accusation or indirectly as a nagging or punitive attack ("Put down your stupid iPhone, for God's sake"); a simpering lament ("You spend more time golfing than you do with me"); a demand ("Stop avoiding me"); or a continual complaint of "You're never around when I need you." But no matter how it emerges, it is often a payback or punishment directed against the one who "loves something more." And rather than driving the couple to more closeness, these responses tend to drive couples farther apart.

These You Love _____ More than Me fights have the right idea but the wrong expression. It's healthy for couples to argue about why one is avoiding the other, either physically or emotionally. Whether the avoidance or absences are from indulging in soft addictions like over-shopping or binge television-watching, avoiding each other because of discomfort with intimacy, staying away for fear of conflict, or trying to numb some upset rather than face it, getting to the bottom of this fight can provide fodder for deeply satisfying lives and deeper, more intimate relationships.

9. Family Feuds

I was appearing on *Oprah* when the legendary, wise television personality threw up her hands, shook her head, and during a break asked me to appear on the show earlier than planned because her guests were behaving so badly. The show was about contentious battling in-laws, and Oprah said, "You handle them!"

Family Feuds happen in numerous ways, including fights about your in-laws' irritating behaviors ("Your mother drives me crazy!"), interference ("If your father butts in one more time, I'll…"), and failure to deal with your parents as they treat your partner badly ("Your mother treats me like crap, and you don't do anything about it!").

Family Feuds are tricky. Allegiances become confused, and battle lines get drawn. Sorting through these battles to the issues underneath can be some of the most enlightening and productive fights you can have. Properly handled, they force you to grow up and become your own person, capable of developing allegiance, bonds, and love with each other. Philosophers and psychologists refer to this as individuating, becoming your own person.

10. Told-You-So's

These disagreements often follow a pattern. Sarcasm comes with the I-told-you-so territory, and it leads nowhere. Everyone makes bad decisions, and no one wants to be reminded of them in a sneering tone. These Told-You-So fights can build a wall between partners or provide a bridge of understanding, deepening the relationship if you can take the discussion beyond the sneering and sarcastic levels.

If you totally avoid Told-You-So fights, you won't assess your relative strengths and weaknesses as a team. In these fights, you may be caught in what Alfred Adler (2009) called the inferiority-superiority complex with one-up/one-down dynamics playing out between you. When you dig deeper beneath the I-told-you-so patterns, you can see the limiting beliefs and the roots of your feelings of inferiority or superiority that play out in your relationship. You can begin to shift your limiting way of thinking, feeling, and acting to affirm yourself and each other to build a stronger relationship and a better partnership.

11. You Always _____, You Never _____

We tend to argue in absolutes: you *always* do this; you *never* do that. In fact, it's rarely "never" and it's seldom "always" in the world of human behavior. Making these accusations sparks a flame of resistance and counterattack. You Always _____, You Never _____ fights often stem from a sense of helplessness about the other meeting your needs or heeding your requests.

The words *always* and *never* are called modal operators—they limit reality and possibilities and can be a trap or a self-fulfilling prophecy. They keep exceptions and change from happening. The minute we put the words *always* or *never* into the fight, it's easy to degenerate into first-grade-type fights: "I do not," "You do too." These fights easily become self-fulfilling prophecies stemming from not really believing that you can get your needs met. These fights also often build up after repeated experiences of trying to communicate upsets and not feeling listened to, or after not getting resolution, or from storing the upsets up until they burst out in a summary statement and dismissal of the other's behavior.

12. Deception Perceptions

Keeping secrets, lying, and broken promises are forms of deception that often trigger painful or even rageful fights. When people discover deceptions, they are furious and have the following types of arguments:

Why didn't you tell me that... "your boss was considering you for a promotion;" "you were taking cash out of our account, cashing in our bonds, and remortgaging the house;" "you applied for a job that would make us move;" "you've been flirting on Facebook;" "you had lunch with your old girlfriend or boyfriend;" "you really don't like my meatloaf..."

You lied to me. "You said you were at a training for work, but Joe said he saw you at the golf outing." "You told me that you were working late, and you went out for drinks with the girls."

Broken promises. "You guaranteed we would get a new kitchen." "You told me we'd never move again." "You swore you wouldn't hang out with your buddies all night." "You promised me you'd check with me before you..." "You promised you'd go on a diet." "You promised me you'd talk to me before you drew money out of that account."

Understanding the nature of the promise, secret, or lie and the underlying reasons for the deception is the goal. The specific lie isn't the issue. Half-hearted or even heartfelt confessions ("I'll be better in the future") aren't the answers here either. What should be the focal point of the argument is trust: why one person feels she or he can't trust the other, and what the couple can do to rebuild that trust. Unearthing the insecurities, areas of distrust, and fears behind these deceptions can be painful but are also very revealing and healing, both individually and for the couple.

13. You're Just Like Your Mother/Father

This often-explosive argument generally cuts to the quick, especially when you have long dreaded being like your mother or father. Your partner plays on this, which is why these are fighting words. But if the argument is only a debate about who's right or whether you really are like that parent, then it will go nowhere. If you're fighting about a specific behavior or attitude you exhibit that is similar to that parent, though, then you can use it to burrow down to a richer, more productive conflict. Maybe you fear that your relationship will be just like that of your parents. Maybe you are exhibiting a parental behavior that you know is destructive, but you're trying to communicate a more profound message to your partner about what's missing in your lives.

Use the mother-father debate as a powerful lens into your past to see its impact on your present relationship—how your upbringing and your relationship with your parents affects you individually and as a couple—and what you can do to change it. Questions that lead to deeper understanding include: What about the behavior that is like your mother or father is problematic for you? What feelings does it evoke? What would you like in its place? What is the desired behavior and outcome you want? You will be dealing with the roots of your pain or anger, and you'll be free to see and love your partner for who he or she is—not just as a projection of your parent or your past.

14. You've Changed/You Won't Change

"You've changed." "Why can't you just be like you used to be?" "You never used to do that." "Were you just faking when we were going out?" or "You won't change." "Why can't you just think ahead?" "You just don't want to change." "You could change if you wanted to." These fights become particularly intense when people see change as the litmus test of love.

Regardless of whether your partner has changed or won't change, you feel hurt, angry, or even betrayed. If you refrain from engaging in an argument about it, that sense of betrayal will linger and can poison the relationship. Confrontation, on the other hand, can lead to resolution in these tricky fights if you negotiate the conflict responsibly. Otherwise, they may become enervating repetitions of "You promised that you would change," "I did not," "You did too." Or, they can devolve into ongoing plaintive moans of "Why can't you just love me the way I am?" or stubborn stances like "It's you who needs to change. I don't want to change; I'm happy"; or "This is who I am; deal with it." Change is threatening, yet necessary for thriving relationships.

15. You Embarrassed Me

Embarrassment comes in many forms. "I can't believe you let everyone know that the doctor told me I should lose twenty-five pounds; I'm so ashamed," or "What made you think that our sex life is anybody else's business? You know how private I am. I am so humiliated."

People embarrass each other all the time in relationships; they say and do things that make the other person cringe. Ignoring these shaming or embarrassing moments leads to worse problems if the underlying issue is never addressed and the shame and embarrassment continue.

On the other hand, genuine inquiry about why you feel ashamed and why the other person behaves in ways that you find so embarrassing can lead to epiphanies and empathy. Teasing out these fights can reveal important elements of each other's values, social mores, and unconscious family rules and beliefs that govern behavior. These fights can also surface blind spots that have been compromising your success or satisfaction. Rather than just trying to manage each other's behavior, you can learn much from each other—ranging from understanding what is underneath your partner's sensitivity to becoming more willing to "break the rules" like your partner and express yourself, even if it bothers others.

The Six Skills of Getting to the Heart of the Fight and Battling to Bliss

No matter what your fight type, our research and experience with successful couples revealed the process to get to the heart of the fight and grow closer through conflict. As you become adept at what we call the Battling to Bliss process—a process that consists of six key relationship skills—you'll fight in ways that help rather than hurt the relationship and that foster the intimacy and fulfillment you seek. Understanding and intimacy through conflict take work, but the benefits are well worth it. Understand that the success depends on you, not your partner. The skills of conflict completion build on one another, but you will apply them uniquely, in sequence or individually. Interpersonal improvements are a result of each of you learning and growing, getting to the roots of the fight, and meeting your underlying unmet needs.

So take responsibility for these skills rather than relying on your partner to be more empathic, understanding, and so on. The best way to take responsibility is by becoming adept at the six key bliss skills. Once you are proficient at using them, you'll fight in ways that help rather than hurt the relationship and that foster the intimacy and fulfillment you seek. We'll detail each of these skills in later chapters but for now, here is a summary.

Skill #1: Yearn

We start by reawakening our moment-by-moment yearning to see and be seen, to touch and be touched, to love and be loved, to matter, to contribute, and to make a difference. Our fights are unconscious attempts to get our unrecognized yearnings met or a protest against them not being met. Great relationships require stepping out of routine and habit, and this skill begins by learning to have our yearning guide us in our interactions. You'll unpack your fights and use what you find to get to the true yearnings underneath. You're blaming him for forgetting you hate cilantro in the dish he's just prepared, but what you really yearn for is for him to acknowledge that you matter.

Skill #2: Engage

Spontaneous, uncensored, in-the-moment responses to yearnings happen when we engage. This often means experimenting with different ways of being together. Once we stop trying to defend ourselves or win the argument and look for the yearning and engage from that, we begin learning about ourselves and each other. You will not only engage in meeting your own yearning, but you will also recognize and meet the yearnings of your partner. By following the rules of engagement, you'll minimize your destructive interactions and maximize your constructive, creative exchanges.

Skill #3: Reveal

Not all goes smoothly as we yearn and engage. The bumps in the road invite us to reflect on what is going on under the surface. We become more aware of ourselves, our inner motivations, and our historic programming and we share more of ourselves. In this skill, you dig down deep to see what is really going on with you—to unearth why certain actions set you off and what they reveal about you and your unfinished business. As you make these discoveries, you share them with your partner. You begin to recognize your *matrix*—the web of neural pathways that encode your early experiences into unconscious limiting attitudes, personal biases, and mistaken beliefs. And as you become aware of these unconscious restrictive beliefs, you begin to recognize the key elements of your matrix that need to be challenged. You find productive ways to be curious about yourself; you become self-reflective and self-confronting. You also seek feedback from others, especially the feedback that comes from your relationship.

Skill #4: Liberate

Stepping out of the cage of habit, doing the undoable, saying the unsayable—liberating is inspired from revealing, just as engaging follows yearning. With this skill you break free of old patterns and step into new ways of being. You experiment with new behaviors and act on your new discoveries of revealing. You challenge your limiting beliefs and discover new possibilities of relating. You share what's really going on with you and break out of traditional battle roles and patterns. Liberating frees you to be more you as you identify skills to develop and create new relationship possibilities. You explore new frontiers of intimacy, learning and growing as individuals and as a couple.

Skill #5: Rematrix

Rematrixing is strategically liberating with the intent to build new neural pathways of empowering beliefs, behaviors, ways of being, and relating. It requires intense, repeated practice to develop firm foundations for these new thoughts, feelings, and actions. With this skill, you learn what it takes to really change your brain, your behavior, and as a result, your relationship. When you consistently rematrix, you keep from slipping backward, and are able to change for the better, forever.

Skill #6: Dedicate

Dedicating, the lifelong commitment to rematrixing, refers to engaging consciously and consistently in your own transformation and becoming the best you can be. When you dedicate, you set up challenges to further stretch yourself all the time. You commit fully to bringing out the best in yourself and your relationship. You are willing to pay the price of discomfort or do whatever it takes to keep yourself learning, growing, and transforming to have a great relationship and life. You bring more of you to your relationship. You find rejuvenation in the newness of the ongoing challenges you address, moving forward and maximizing your enjoyment, engagement, development, and contribution to your world.

The Courage to Fight for Something

You're not going into battle empty-handed; the six skills will serve you well in all types of relationship fights in which you engage. But even armed with the skills, you need to exhibit bravery as you bicker over small things and battle over big issues. To bolster your courage, remember that you're fighting for something meaningful—a relationship that can rise to the level of bliss.

We are thrilled that you are joining us on the journey. You will discover how fully engaged couples operate when they believe that relationships can be robust, growing adventures. The couples you'll meet in the following chapters are concerned not with appearances but with genuine, full-bodied interaction in the pursuit of great relationships. As you join them, you will learn how to use relationship conflict to create deeper, more fulfilling relationships—deeper and more fulfilling than you ever imagined.

The first step in the process involves acknowledging and understanding a truth that will help you grasp the value of and reasons for relationship fights: *love is messy.*

CHAPTER 2

Love Is Messy

True love isn't about running in slow motion across a field of wild-flowers into each other's arms and murmuring sweet nothings into each other's ears. Nor is it about being on a never-ending honeymoon and existing in a perpetual state of ecstatic union where every day is sunny and we engage in perfectly synchronized, effortless, multiple-orgasmic, no-sweat, no-fart sex.

True love means you both dig in the dirt of the relationship and pull the weeds to create an ever-growing intimacy. It means kissing and yelling, playing and fighting, comforting and challenging each other. It means being real, not careful. If you want true love, you will need to feel everything: the fear, hurt, anger, and sadness, as well as joy and bliss.

So love is messy. Why are we telling you this? Because only when you wrap your head around the messiness that is at the heart of intimate relationships can you appreciate why conflict is necessary. As you'll dis-cover, having fights doesn't guarantee a great marriage or partnership. You need to learn why and how and when to fight, and what to fight about. You need to figure out how to use everything from petty squabbles to big blowout arguments to

- be understood;
- understand your partner;
- get what you want;
- enjoy the adventure;

- learn and grow together;

- get closer and be more intimate.

Engaging in conflict that builds intimacy takes practice. Because love is messy, some people avoid fights to avoid dealing with the messiness. Because love is a complex, volatile mix, other people engage in destructive conflict—they play games, they fight mindlessly, they argue with one foot in the past and one in the present. We're going to help you learn how to engage in relationship fights with this messiness in mind so you can battle to bliss rather than into divorce court.

If you are already an all-out fighter, then this book will help you use conflict more productively; you'll figure out how to get to the heart of the fight and share that with your partner to become closer. If you are a conflict avoider who thinks anger is a harbinger of relationship doom, you'll learn skills to engage in arguments that catalyze both your personal growth and your growth as a couple, bringing you more intimacy and closeness.

If all this seems counterintuitive, it's because love is neither logical nor linear. Instead, it's volatile, unpredictable, and governed by primal forces that are buried deep inside of us. This is powerful, messy stuff. But it's stuff you can and should understand, and the key to understanding is developing the capacity to responsibly clash over issues that are important to you. If you can't do that—if you act as if a loving relationship is a predictable, rational progression that mirrors movie romance—then you'll remain mired. You may never fight, but you also won't grow, and neither will the relationship.

It's only when you really and truly engage with another person—and by engaging we mean being totally honest, responsible, and open in verbal and emotional communication—that truths emerge. All the fight types—from the Blame Game to Family Feuds and Told-You-So's—foster thought-provoking conversations, valuable insights, and even the occasional epiphany. We'll talk about how to use these fight types in beneficial ways, but first, let's look at what the research says about how good fights produce great relationships.

Digging into the Mess

Couples don't get divorced because they fight; they split up because they don't know how to use conflict to create a new depth of intimacy—which would never occur without working through these challenges. The point is not to avoid a fight, or to find a formula to get through a fight, or even to win a fight, but rather to dig in and discover the rich information beneath the argument. Yes, you're going to get down and dirty, but studies show that relationships benefit when you explore what resides beneath the surface.

Emerging relationship research proves that couples who have truthful, angry fights early in their relationship are happier over time. Social psychology researcher James McNulty has found that the "short-term discomfort of an angry but honest conversation" is beneficial to relationships in the long run (Prigg 2012). As you'll discover, relationships are stronger than you think. They can withstand the fireballs of argument; more to the point, heated exchanges can catalyze the insight and understanding that foster relationship growth.

Other studies show that conflict early in the relationship helps couples weed out problems that can damage the relationship in the long run. John Gottman's (1994, 66) research indicates that the "temporary misery" of early conflict is healthier for couples in the long term. Interestingly, in the early years of relationships, peaceful couples report that they are happier than bickering couples, but when revisited three years later, the peaceful couples are far more likely to be divorced or on their way to breaking up (Gottman 1994). The couples who worked out their issues are more likely to be in stable relationships.

You're going to meet some couples throughout this book whose scorched-earth battles make you swear they couldn't possibly still be together. You'll find that though they appeared to have made a mess of their early years, they were simply fighting to understand each other and raise the relationship to a higher level.

Life = Conflict

So let's not kid ourselves and look at the reality. *Everyone* has conflict. EVERYONE. Conflict is a fact of an engaged life. As each dance partner does his or her own steps, they step on each other's toes. In order to get really good at relationship, we need to bump into each other. If he wants to see an action flick and you want to see a romance, and you avoid mentioning your desire and go to the action flick, that's conflict. If she likes to save money and you like to spend it, and you both silently fume at the other's money habits, that's conflict. Conflict comes up every time you have a different desire, opinion, or viewpoint—which, if you are honest and engaged, is often. It's everywhere. Dealing with it productively is what brings you closer, and not dealing with it, or dealing with it unproductively, puts distance between you.

Evolutionary biologist Elisabet Sahtouris (2000) points out that conflict is part of life, beginning at the cellular level. Mitosis, the process of cell division, is a continual cycle of conflict and resolution. A cell begins as one, but this original sense of unity is broken as it divides into two, competing for available resources and creating tension, until a new union or harmony is formed. And then they divide again, creating a new tension in the quest for available resources until another union is formed, beginning ongoing cycles of unity, tension, diversity, and new harmony. Similarly, your relationship is a constantly growing organism marked by alternating conflict and unity. For the relationship to keep growing, things need to keep breaking apart and reforming.

You will come to see your conflict as a natural part of the growth process in the relationship—and how the unrecognized struggle between your opposing urges for togetherness and individuality keeps you either stuck in circular fights or not openly engaging at all. Family systems theorist Murray Bowen (1993) posits that we all have opposing, and equally compelling, urges to merge for togetherness, on the one hand, and on the other, to separate and have our individuality, what he calls differentiating. You will learn to honor, accept, and powerfully integrate these drives. You will see how effectively negotiating these drives creates healthy, close relationships—you unite even more powerfully while maintaining a strong, distinct, and solid sense of self.

Fighting for Our Life

Evolutionary science shows us that our connection with others is what kept us alive in prehistoric as well as more recent times. For early humans, having relationships increased their ability to hunt, gather food, and provide protection from predators—it wasn't a luxury to have relationships; it was a necessity for survival (Hart and Sussman 2005). We evolved to equate survival with having relationships.

Neuroscientists have found that social fear and social pain are associated with the loss or threatened loss of a loved one, and these centers are wired in the same areas of the brain as physical pain, which is why we experience the fear and pain so viscerally and profoundly (Lieberman 2013). When our connection to our loved one is threatened or we lose a relationship, it activates a primal fear—we experience it (unconsciously) as a threat to our survival—triggering a response of fight, flight, or freeze.

You will learn about couples who avoided fights as if their lives depended on it—unconsciously, this was a justifiable, evolutionary-based fear. You will also encounter couples who battled with such intensity, frequency, and volume that it too seemed a matter of survival—and to them, again unconsciously, that's exactly what it was.

In the next section, we'll leave the realm of research for a close-up look at a couple who became tangled up in the mess of their love for each other and maintained an eerie and enervating peace.

Battling Back from the Brink

Why do some couples find ways to avoid ever getting in shouting matches or even openly disagreeing? Many people harbor false assumptions about relationship battles and their roles and repercussions. They may have grown up observing horrendous, abusive battles between their parents or been seduced by Hollywood's notion of romance; they are enchanted by the impossible romantic ideal of relationships where an unkind word is never spoken, where passion never fades, and where they live happily ever after. Here's the story of one couple who started out attempting to submerge all conflict.

Doug and Deneen were on the brink of divorce. Like many couples, they thought they had fallen out of love after years together, a common mis-analysis. What had started out as a promising partnership full of hope had degenerated into a peaceful but pernicious coexistence.

Now Deneen would be on her own for the first time in her life. All she needed to do was pay the security deposit on the apartment she had found. For the first time in her life since college, she would be living without Doug. She was afraid, but she felt ready for the challenge; it was better than his irritatingly passive, nonexpressive presence. She'd long ago determined she would never want to have a child with him.

Doug was feeling desperate. Not only was he hurt and alone, but his upset feelings were preoccupying him throughout the day and he was making errors at work that had cost him a potential partnership. He was failing everywhere.

Similar to many couples who once were deeply in love, they decided to make one last-ditch effort before ending the relationship. They began working with us and learning how to engage anew. Deneen realized how she had been trying to keep their marriage "nice," but that meant that she had actually been withholding herself, her judgments, and even her wishes and desires from Doug. By not expressing herself or her needs, she had been growing more and more dissatisfied and unhappy until she thought she had to move out. Doug realized that he didn't fight for what he wanted or ask for the support or encouragement he deserved. He had not challenged himself or Deneen to engage in the relationship.

They realized they were enmeshed in two types of fights, the first of which was a subtle form of You've Changed/You Won't Change.

Deneen complained that Doug no longer adored her. She wondered if he had been faking it originally. She silently stewed in her hurt and wondered why he couldn't just be like he used to be.

She would ask him questions about his satisfaction, hoping he would show some concern for the relationship, but he always said he was "fine with it." Though her anger was roiling inside and every so often would erupt, she tried to avoid the battles that reminded her of the "scary" arguments her parents used to have.

Recognize This?   Does this muted type of conflict feel familiar? Are you convinced that your partner is not the same person he was at the start of the relationship? Do you find yourself growing distant from the person you thought you loved but who increasingly seems like a stranger? Are you angry inside but trying to maintain your cool in the hope that somehow, some way, the relationship will return to "normal"? If so, chances are you're burying your upset and avoiding conflict or are engaged in some passive-aggressive behavior such as Hidden Middle Finger fights.

If you act like Deneen and refrain from engaging in an argument about how your partner has changed, you'll feel betrayed; that feeling will linger and can poison the relationship.

Confrontation, on the other hand, can lead to resolution. But these You've Changed/You Won't Change fights are tricky—part of love's messy essence.

Love would be a less messy business if we only had to worry about one fight type. Unfortunately, we often become enmeshed in a number of different types of fights. Doug and Deneen, for instance, also had Hidden Middle Finger battles when they expressed dissatisfaction indirectly. For example, Deneen felt that refusing to cook what Doug would like would communicate that she didn't appreciate him not cleaning up after himself. Each was silently thinking, *That ought to show him/her,* but it never got through to either of them that flipping a subtle middle finger fails to resolve issues or deepen the relationship.

Getting the hidden middle finger out in the open is critical. Doug and Deneen, like most couples stuck in this fight, just didn't have much social-emotional intelligence. Over time and with practice, however, they learned to express their feelings (beyond their middle finger) and interact more truthfully with each other. This learning began when they realized that they were being similarly indirect at work and that each of them was stagnating professionally. It started to dawn on them that neither of them was growing personally, either, and they both were feeling trapped. As they began to understand the dynamics of their passive and covert fights, they saw how their patterns had kept each of them stuck and that their patterns wouldn't just go away by leaving the relationship.

Collecting and compounding their unrecognized hurts and resentments was driving them apart. They learned to see how these hurts originated from deep needs that weren't being met. Like kids tiptoeing into cold water at the beach, they began taking tentative steps to communicate what those needs were and how the other might meet them. It wasn't easy—they segued from passive conflict to vociferous verbal disagreements—but they also began communicating with and affirming each other. The fights helped them connect. They had plenty of past hurts to catch up on as they learned the skills of responsible communication, and eventually they were able to cool down quickly after arguments, find a genuine calm and connectedness, and focus better on what really matters.

They each began to stretch themselves, to escape old stagnating patterns, to embrace new experiences, and to accept change. Subsequently, both of them had career breakthroughs as they rediscovered each other and achieved a greater degree of intimacy—greater even than when they first fell in love. And through this growth process, Deneen and Doug fought fairly, intensely, and with ever-increasing levels of communication, self-knowledge, and trust. As they dug into their unconscious patterns, they realized that they both saw people as fragile and mistakenly believed that conflict was sure to destroy relationships.

In the course of their work with us, they came to understand how they had avoided uncomfortable topics and showing their feelings. As they developed deeper trust in each other, they actually liked the aliveness that came with their disagreements. They also developed a new empowering vision for what their relationship could be.

If all relationships were like Doug and Deneen's, then we could create a single formula for how to battle to bliss and get to the heart of the fight. But as you no doubt are aware, relationships are tremendously complex, and couples create different ways of both avoiding fights and engaging in them. Though the process we'll introduce in part 2 applies to all couples no matter what their fight types might be, you need to be aware of the particular way in which you become engaged in relationship squabbles (or the particular way you deal with conflict through denial, passivity, and so on).

This self-awareness is essential, since the only way you can sort through the messy details of a relationship is by understanding your specific messy emotions and behaviors when conflicts arise. To help you gain this understanding, we introduced you to Doug and Deneen, who practiced fight-avoidance behaviors. Now, we want to introduce you to another couple who fought all the time but in the wrong way.

Going in Circles, Caught in a Triangle

Collin and Edie loved each other, but both agreed that her fiery temper led to explosive fights; she took the offensive, and he became defensive or sought refuge in his claim of superior intellectual perspective. Collin loved her aliveness, and she valued his solidity, but they were never sure if their relationship was "the one." Though they couldn't imagine separating, they also feared making a commitment they could not keep. They discussed with friends the indecisiveness that was making their relationship messy, and then one friend became fed up with their attitude and suggested they "shit or get off the pot." This friend referred them to us, and they recognized they needed help; neither of them wanted to have the kind of relationship that their parents had, marked by divorce as well as violence.

Collin and Edie talked about how their relationship battles involved screaming, throwing things, and stomping out of the room. Collin criticized Edie for her irrationality, dodging the truth, and sloppy housekeeping. Edie was enraged by Collin's "tight-assed way of being" and his "superior way of looking down on her." Their fights were textbook examples of the Blame Game, the Deception Perception, and the less common variation on the Blame Game, You're Crazy.

"You're crazy!" Collin would shout at Edie as she unleashed her litany of complaints about him. Collin blamed Edie's dissatisfaction on her craziness, and Edie blamed her dissatisfaction on Collin.

Collin was the first to see how getting caught in the Blame Game meant he was trapped in what transactional analysts call the drama triangle—the interaction pattern where people indirectly attempt to meet interpersonal needs by assuming the role of victim, rescuer, or persecutor, and avoid taking appropriate responsibility (Karpman 1968). Edie assumed the persecutor role until Collin retaliated with his hurtful claim that she was "crazy." He would then move from the victim to persecutor. Collin began as the white knight rescuer—setting himself up to be blamed for any dissatisfaction—and Edie began as a rescued victim, a perfect foundational basis to become his persecutor for having failed to "make her happy." Sound familiar? The plot of every soap opera and drama revolves around these roles, too, which might explain why we get so hooked by them—they externalize our inner process.

These dramas perpetuate themselves in endless loops of dissatisfaction with no real change due to the indirect attempts to fulfill legitimate human yearnings. And, too often, they result in deteriorating relationships. The way out? Collin and Edie began taking responsibility for their own experiences. This means they began recognizing the deeper yearning that they each felt and engaging in responsible, heartfelt communication. As they got at what was really going on underneath the blame and feelings of victimhood, they discovered new levels of creative problem solving and positive results.

Like many couples, Collin and Edie didn't just engage in one type of fight. Besides the Blame Game, they were also struggling with Deception Perception battles. Keeping secrets, lying, and broken promises are forms of deception that often trigger painful or even rage-filled fights. Edie felt Collin was hiding his shortcomings, and Collin was frequently enraged at Edie for reporting only partial information, leaving out key aspects of events.

Collin and Edie both felt betrayed and blamed the other until each recognized the roots of these feelings. Collin's father's faithlessness in his marriage and Edie's family's frequent unwillingness to pay debts created the expectation of betrayal. As they uncovered these and other truths about their relationship, Collin and Edie began to replace blame with personal responsibility. Conflicts became starting points for deeper inquiry and mutuality and for explorations of why there was a lack of trust and what could be done to rebuild that trust.

Examining the foundations of their union, Collin realized he loved Edie's wild side and how she provided relief from his uptight family of origin. In turn, Edie discovered that she yearned for the stability Collin offered, that he represented the solid, respectable existence that contrasted starkly with her own family's peripatetic nature and financial instability. Through their more productive arguments, they both became more like each other; Edie became more solid, and Collin became more spontaneous and fun. Best of all, they both learned to fight full-out and become closer through their differences. Through the years they have empowered one another to be their best. Collin has become a stellar executive in a fast-moving company, and Edie went back to school and has become a national prize-winning designer operating her own business.

Do you avoid fighting like Doug and Deneen did? Are you full-out emotional fighters like Collin and Edie, where your fights are often destructive or never seem to go anywhere? Are you somewhere in between? Or is one of you an avoider and the other a full-out fighter? Conflict styles are not pure, so you may possess traits of different types. See what elements define your current conflict style by taking this quiz.

HOW DO YOU DEAL WITH THE MESS?

Think back to your last few fights, conflicts, or upsets. Which of the following describe aspects of your fights (or your avoidance of fighting)? Check the box or boxes after each item to indicate whether it is a usual behavior you or your partner exhibit.

	Me	My Partner
1. Yelling	☐	☐
2. Mix of angry outbursts with humor or compassion	☐	☐
3. Pulling away	☐	☐
4. Really listening to my partner and trying to understand his or her point of view	☐	☐
5. Silent treatment	☐	☐
6. Insulting the other (name calling, sarcasm, hostile humor, mockery)	☐	☐
7. Changing the subject	☐	☐
8. Telling the truth	☐	☐
9. Belligerence	☐	☐
10. Bringing up things that happened long ago	☐	☐
11. Resolving the fight	☐	☐
12. Expressing my feelings	☐	☐
13. Validating my partner's points (letting my partner know I understand his or her point)	☐	☐
14. Quiet but smug, icy, superior	☐	☐
15. Getting to what was really bugging me and expressing it	☐	☐

16. Demanding to have the last word or making my points, not really listening to my partner	☐	☐
17. Contempt (attacking; hostile words, tone of voice, or gestures; eye rolling; sneering; and so forth)	☐	☐
18. Getting what is really going on with my partner and understanding his or her feelings	☐	☐
19. Escalating with no resolution	☐	☐
20. Leaving the discussion or fight, walking away	☐	☐
21. Counterattacking	☐	☐
22. Defensiveness (excuses; cross complaining; disagreeing and then counterattacking; yes, buts...)	☐	☐
23. Withdrawing	☐	☐
24. Disengaging	☐	☐
25. Acknowledging my responsibility in the fight	☐	☐
26. Getting quiet (or mumbling)	☐	☐
27. Avoiding the fight	☐	☐

Scoring

You are engaging in aspects of *destructive conflict* if you checked 1, 6, 9, 10, 16, 17, 19, 21, and 22. It's your fight style, not your actual fights, that can damage your relationship. Hostility, contempt, and defensiveness not only keep you from resolving fights, but also create ill will and distance. Explosive fighting itself—yelling, for example—isn't the problem. It's the degree of belligerence and contempt that creates distance. In fact, as you learn to add humor and compassion to your explosive style, your fights will become more constructive.

You are *avoiding conflict* if you checked 3, 5, 7, 14, 20, 23, 24, 26, and 27. Avoiding, withdrawing, and stonewalling mark your conflict style, which is also destructive. By avoiding conflict, issues aren't addressed, resentment builds, true feelings and needs aren't surfaced, and distance and distrust result. While you may be trying to avoid the tension and upset of fighting, withdrawal signals a lack of commitment to the relationship and unwillingness to work things out. This is especially problematic if one of you is an avoider and the other is a constructive fighter—one wants to fix things and the other one wants to leave.

You practice aspects of *constructive conflict* if you checked 2, 4, 8, 11, 12, 13, 15, 18, and 25. You are able to express your feelings and desires and to see and hear your partner's point of view and his or her feelings; you're also able to resolve your fights more often than not. You may argue fiercely and at high volumes, but you are often able to work things through using humor, affection, and positive engagement.

Whether or not you had a predominant type, each instance you checked of destructive conflict or avoiding conflict is an opportunity to move toward more constructive conflicts.

Surprisingly, explosive fighters aren't the most toxic or damaging (Birditt et al. 2010). The most dangerous pattern is when one partner is engaged in relating and working on a problem and the other withdraws. The mixed pattern of a fighter and an avoider significantly lessens the probable longevity of a marriage, not to mention fulfillment within it.

Whatever your fight styles, you'll learn more about these patterns, where they come from, and what skills you'll need to battle to bliss in the chapters that follow.

The Benefits of Getting Down and Dirty

As you can see from the stories of Collin and Edie and Doug and Deneen, achieving a great relationship isn't a simple or fast process. Like love itself, it's filled with ambiguity, volatility, and unpredictability. You need to be willing to learn how to fight fairly, and as our two couples demonstrate, this means speaking honestly, critically, and at times, painfully. But we can promise that you'll be more than compensated for your effort. Intimacy, joy, and even transcendence are common outcomes of battling to bliss and getting to the heart of the fight, and you and your partner can enjoy these outcomes together.

More specifically, what follows are the benefits that you'll receive if you learn to battle to bliss, see love as the messy thing it is, and engage in the process that recognizes the realities of love.

First, you'll learn and grow in a dynamic, resilient relationship that becomes stronger as you become more aware of yourself and develop your relationship conflict skills. You'll discover how to heal hurts within the relationship as well as to experiment with new, relationship-building behaviors.

Second, you'll live a life of adventure and understanding when you resolve your battles. Even better, in the wake of this resolution you'll experience true intimacy. You will come to understand your partner and feel closer than ever before. Like soldiers, when you both enter a battle together and survive, the bond between you strengthens. You know why certain things matter to your partner that you never really understood before—why he's so obsessive about being on time, for instance, and how his unfinished business triggered the fight (he grew up in a household where everyone was always late and often missed important events—he becomes furious when your tardiness causes you both to arrive late).

Third, you'll become more empathic and celebrate the person you love. This is not only about understanding but also *feeling* who that other person is—what drives her, what bedevils him. During the argument, you will both express feelings that are more honest and direct than ones you've ever expressed to each other. You will feel his hurt, and he will feel yours. This is an emotionally electric experience. Conflict takes on immediacy, and more of each of you is engaged. You will share more. The conflicts may take longer to resolve, but the time spent will deepen and broaden the relationship.

Fourth, you will learn to trust your partner and yourself in ways that never seemed possible before. You will both see that you're tougher than you thought, that the other person's fragility was an illusion. You'll stop walking on eggshells to avoid certain topics; you'll also stop using a sledgehammer to make your points. As a more powerful trust develops, you'll realize that you can survive any verbal argument and that the relationship can thrive in its wake. This allows you both to stay with issues more fully and explore how the conflict affects you.

You'll also be in a great position to identify the myths and misconceptions that prevent couples from engaging in the messy fights that elevate relationships. As you're about to find out, people stay away from productive arguments or engage in them poorly because they subscribe to beliefs that have the ring of truth but are in fact destructive illusions.

CHAPTER 3

Happily Never After

Getting Past Fairy-Tale Romance
So You Can Fight for True Love

J ust about everything we've ever learned about relationships doesn't work. From children's stories to grandmothers' advice to even some professional advice, much of what we have been told about relationships has not been helpful, and in many cases, is even harmful.

In the fairy tales, Prince Charming mounts his snow-white steed and embarks on a quest to find the beautiful princess. After great difficulty, he rescues her and they ride off into the sunset to live happily ever after. In these types of tales, love conquers all. With the kiss of the princess, a frog turns into a prince; the beast is saved through the love of the beauty; and with enough love and support, the chore-girl Cinderella is transformed into a princess.

These relationship myths are uber-misconceptions—a type grounded in powerful cultural images that become deeply embedded in our unconscious mind, influencing our relationships and setting us up for disappointment, bitterness, resentment, despair, and any number of fights when our life doesn't look like the fairy tales and our unconscious, magical expectations are dashed.

And it doesn't stop with fairy tales. The cultural barrage of television, psychobabble, popular songs, romance novels, and other culprits conspire to create or reinforce other relationship misconceptions—the prostitute is made an honest woman and marries the billionaire, the factory working girl is carried out of the sweatshop by her handsome transformed military officer, and a host of other romance stories in the same vein. These, coupled with conflicting professional advice, old wives' tales, and poor relationship role models, all contribute to the misinformation, mistaken guidance, and just plain lies we've learned about relationships.

RELATIONSHIP FACTS QUIZ

True or False?

1. The purpose of a relationship is to make you happier.	T	F
2. Being with the right person makes you happier.	T	F
3. True love means you are accepted the way you are.	T	F
4. It's important to help your partner change in ways that matter to you.	T	F
5. Soul mates make the best relationships.	T	F
6. You know when you meet "the one."	T	F
7. If it is the right relationship, things work out.	T	F
8. If a relationship is too hard, it's probably not the right one.	T	F
9. Chemistry is very important in a relationship.	T	F
10. Attraction is very important in a relationship.	T	F
11. Incompatibility and conflict are signs of a poor match.	T	F
12. It's important to have a lot in common and be compatible in a relationship.	T	F
13. You are either compatible, or you're not.	T	F
14. A successful relationship is mostly a matter of finding a compatible partner right from the start.	T	F
15. Relationships that do not start off well inevitably fail.	T	F
16. Love is all you need.	T	F

17. If it's true love, it should be easy.		T	F
18. It's important to be turned on by your partner.		T	F
19. When the "thrill is gone," it's a sign that you are falling out of love.		T	F
20. If you fall out of love, it means you were in the wrong relationship.		T	F

SCORING

Count your *true* choices. If you answered *true* to any of the questions above, you are under the influence of relationship misconceptions. These are all relationship myths that limit intimacy and keep you from lasting, satisfying, fulfilling, intimate relationships. The higher your ratio of true to false, the more you buy the mythology. Read on to discover the truth about lasting, fulfilling relationships.

Relationship Myths and Misconceptions

Never underestimate the power of myths to undermine relationship success. These larger-than-life cultural beliefs are uber-misconceptions, embedded in our collective unconsciousness through childhood stories, fairy tales, movies, and other fictions. Studies show that Cinderella and similar fairy-tale elements are present in 78 percent of people's beliefs about romantic love, which lead to unnecessary disillusionment, angst, and even devastation in relationships (Lockhart 2000).

Garden-variety misconceptions may lack the power of the unconscious or the force of a cultural belief, but they are no less insidious. As assumptions that masquerade as truths, they can influence our relationship behaviors in countless ways.

Both serve as obstacles to blissful relationships, and they cause us to make relationship mistakes such as avoiding potentially useful conflict ("I thought conflict was bad, and we were supposed to be happy"). Or we engage in destructive battles without resolution, thinking there is something wrong with us or our partner ("I'm right; she's wrong"). Until we identify these myths and misconceptions and learn to move past them, we can't fight productively or fairly. Most couples don't live happily ever after. Almost half of all marriages end in divorce. Remarkably, we persist in pursuing old models of relationships in which hopeful couples keep falling in love, but too few have a happy ending.

What's wrong with this picture? We try to achieve an ideal relationship that is not only impossible, but also not even desirable! Living happily ever after implies unexamined, unconscious, static ways of being. Living happily ever after isn't the point. Living *deeply ever after* is what matters.

Happily ever after leaves no room for tough times. It leads us to sidestep problems to avoid upset and discord, or to fear that our conflict means we've made the wrong choice. We try to live up to an ideal rather than living in the messy but fulfilling reality. We avoid fighting, become careful and dishonest, even fake, with each other. We limit our expression so things stay "nice." And when we are not nice, when we drop the façade of carefulness, we have no idea how to argue productively.

If we do fight, these encounters are often accompanied by a sense of despair. We worry that we have made a mistake, that we got into a relationship with the wrong person or even worse, with some sort of monster. The happily-ever-after fantasy spawns inauthentic, superficial relationships or creates anger and heartache when our daily reality doesn't match our fantasy. These fantasies and wishful thoughts are sapping the life out of our relationships, contributing to unresolved fighting, disillusionment, and even divorce.

If you want to live happily ever after, you don't want enough. Happily ever after disregards many meaningful moments—from little joys like appreciating the warmth of your partner's skin as you stroke her face to experiencing comfort in times when you are scared, hurt, or bathed in full tears of joy. It doesn't permit you to be passionately angry about some injustice or to grieve a loss. It misses the depth of intimacy that comes from resolving conflict, being comforted in your pain by your partner, and developing trust by exposing your hurts and fears to another.

So what can you do? You can learn to let go of the fairy tale and live deeply ever after, even if that means getting angry and calling your fairy-tale prince a frog.

Getting Your Relationship Into and Out of the Woods

Couples often come to us saying that they want to be happy, yet their concept is about as developed as the end of a fairy tale—a dreamy, imagined future state based on past happiness and former hormonal lust. Their vague desire for "happiness" is really an unconscious desire to avoid discomfort and the growing pains of living a full life. They think there is something wrong with their relationship because they're arguing constantly with their partner or because they find that they have fallen out of love or gotten turned on by someone other than their partner, and they fear these normal challenges mean the story is over, ruined, or impossible because their experience diverges from the illusory "happiness" they imagined.

They are shocked when we tell them they are right on track, that their disillusionment and conflict are necessary for real, successful relationships to develop. They are at the doorway of great possibility. They must, however, go into the wilderness of the unknown and face uncertainty in order to undo the fairy tale, to help the relationship grow. The Stephen Sondheim musical *Into the Woods* illustrates this point perfectly.

The first act of the musical creatively intertwines fairy tales: Cinderella, Rapunzel, Little Red Riding Hood, Jack and the Beanstalk. In the first act, the fairy tales play out according to our expectations— Jack finds great wealth after climbing the beanstalk, Cinderella marries her prince, Rapunzel is rescued from her tower, Red Riding Hood is saved from the wolf, and their wishes are all fulfilled. The stage is set for them all to live happily ever after.

The second act opens with the audience in a dreamy state, lulled by the happily-ever-after outcomes in the first act. Surprisingly, we find each character discontent and wishing for something else. Cinderella feels empty and seeks meaning by planning a festival. Her Prince Charming is disillusioned and bored with her and her desires, wishing he had quested after Sleeping Beauty instead. Henpecked, Rapunzel's prince is likewise distancing himself from the emotional, distraught Rapunzel, a new mother with a little baby evoking memories of the cruelties experienced at the hands of her evil witch mother. Little Red Riding Hood despairs over the death of her grandmother, and they all wander aimlessly into the woods where terrifying primal forces lurk.

Chaos reigns, and the narrator is killed, meaning that they are no longer in the prewritten fairy tale and they have to write their own stories. This is the critical turning point in the play as they are left in the unknown, dependent on their own and each other's resources.

More to the point, this is the critical moment for couples. This is when they leave the myths of relationship behind and are free to go into the dark woods of their feelings, their beliefs, and their unconscious minds. It is at this point that they can find themselves and each other. Free of the myths, they don't have to pretend that everything is great and can engage in growth-producing conflict. Unburdened by the need to maintain a perfect relationship, they can express their true feelings and argue for their beliefs. This is the point where they begin to write their own love story, letting go of idyllic relationship misconceptions and creating meaning, purpose, and genuine connected intimacy in their relationship. As we've pointed out, this is a lot messier than the myths, but it can help create a deep, meaningful, real, intimate relationship.

Into the Woods was inspired by child psychologist and researcher Bruno Bettelheim (1976), who protested that by homogenizing fairy tales—taking out the monsters, abandonment, death, witches, injuries, and the darkness—we actually deprive children of the opportunity to create a deep inner life, to grapple with the fears and problems they will face in life, and to develop a sense of meaning and purpose.

In the musical, the characters face sobering reality after resisting it. Cinderella finds meaning without her prince. Little Red Riding Hood realizes that she must grow up and face life on her own terms without her mother and grandmother, and Jack realizes that he, too, must chart his own course without family after losing his mother. This is the journey of each member of a couple who battles to bliss—they must go into the woods, beyond fairy tale endings and family myths.

The same is true for couples who subscribe to sanitized fictions about love. The image of meeting "the one," getting married, and then living happily ever after must be replaced. They must go into the dark, face the unknown, and successfully negotiate the chaos and confusion of melding their lives.

We resist seeing the journey into the woods as necessary, clinging to magical solutions. We believe something is wrong when the inevitable conflicts arise, that we need to find a better partner or that our relationship is doomed. We have few models or stories of grappling with the conflicts and challenges of relationships in a way that helps us to grapple with our own. We haven't been shown the path and the process of going into the woods to develop our inner lives, to grapple with the dark forces, and to develop our character and substance. It is in the woods that we forge deep intimacy as well as meaning and purpose.

The bliss skills and process you will learn will help you navigate the trackless paths as you go into the woods where you will venture and develop mature, genuinely happy, responsible ways of being. When you do this, you become more independent and increasingly capable of deep intimacy, standing on your own two feet as full-fledged partners.

We're going to help you travel safely with a guide to make these discoveries. While there, you'll see and accept the parts of yourself you wished to keep hidden, discover even more beauty in your partner, and experience intimacy and bliss previously inconceivable. We're going to help you explore the depth of your relationship, not just the surface. There is no simple technique for lasting results. Your fights can't get resolved on the surface. Think of how often we are shocked to hear that "the ideal couple" has called it quits. They looked good, but the underlying issues were never addressed. Surface resolutions can be likened to rearranging the deck chairs on the *Titanic*. The deck looks great as the ship sinks.

It is often challenging for couples to forsake the comforts of fairy-tale solutions, but the discomfort of letting go is worth paying the price of disturbance, as the story of Riley and Geena demonstrates next. Riley and Geena exchanged the illusory happily-ever-after myths for the realities of emotional friction and genuine intimacy. Facing these discomforts and more, they re-created their relationship in dynamic ways that are still deeply satisfying—more satisfying and productive than the surface pleasures that living the myth provided them. Here's their story. It opens with them living an illusory, idyllic life as if they had been created by Central Casting.

A "Perfect" Couple Who Went Into the Woods

Geena and Riley were living the happily-ever-after fairy tale. She was the pretty princess who married Riley, the handsome Prince Charming. They were the "ideal" couple. They had it all—the perfect house, the perfect clothes, and the start of the perfect family. But, like so many fairy tales, the surface belied the deeper reality.

Their initial devotion to each other diminished over time; she complained that he was insufferably cocky and distant, and he found her aloof and uninterested in sex. They were growing apart, and he was contemplating an affair. They were mired in Sexual Dissatisfaction and If You Really Loved Me, You'd _____ fights, and their arguments began with salvos such as "You are never in the mood!" to "If you really loved me you would want to have sex with me." Occasionally, he complained, "You're just going through the motions."

When we began working with Riley and Geena, they saw us as a last-ditch attempt to save their relationship. At first, they harbored the faint hope that we might restore their happily-ever-after mindset. We quickly disabused them of that notion and began to help them see that their problems were a direct result of them both buying into that myth. We helped them think about "what was wrong with this picture"—how they had assumed that their honeymoon period would last forever, that they were so perfectly matched that all flaws could be overlooked or overcome, and that the passion and devotion that characterized their initial months together would never waver. We talked about how this fairy-tale view of relationships didn't exist in the real world.

Once Riley and Geena were able to get past the happily-ever-after myth, they learned to examine their fights over sexual intimacy and love to discover valuable information. They began to see all types of interaction as intercourse. They realized that lovemaking was not only in the bed, but in how they made the bed. Everything from buying furniture to cooking became opportunities to develop relationship closeness. And sex got better too. In order to do this, they redefined what made relationships good. It was difficult initially for them to see. Talking and arguing about difficult subjects had been painful. They had experienced some vicious arguments and needed to reenter these past battlegrounds in order to apply the bliss skills. They learned to identify when discussions and fights were destructive and undermined the self-confidence of each of them.

They followed the process you will learn in the following chapters, starting by examining their deeper yearning and desires. Riley saw how he yearned for a great deal more than sex. Work was hard, and he often came home dispirited and wanted intercourse to make him feel better. Geena yearned for him to really see and appreciate her instead of using her as a tension reliever. Identifying yearning was the first phase of their journey moving through the woods. Fights still happened, but they were able to dig underneath.

They were amazed at what they found, how talking about basic hungers in a responsible fashion deepened their level of intimacy and took their conversations beyond the cleanliness of the house and the number of times they had sex weekly (even though their sexual activity and satisfaction increased). They were amazed to discover how following their yearnings and engaging, the second bliss skill, took them to much more honest if sometimes painful discussions. To their amazement, they experienced mutual affirmation in fights. The honesty and responsibility in conflicts was satisfying in itself. Often, after a fight, they found themselves falling asleep lovingly in each other's arms feeling closer than they would have with their previously disconnected sexual intercourse. They found that all interactions—whether verbal or physical—became more fulfilling, and their relationship deepened.

This led them to the third step of the process, revealing aspects of their pasts that had resulted in limiting beliefs and revealing more of themselves to one another. They went into the woods and discovered their misleading myths had formed from much deeper family of origin programming. In his unhappiness, Riley had been contemplating an affair. Underneath this, he found a limiting belief, which he could track back generations, that the men in his family believed that women would never please them. Geena uncovered similar limiting beliefs about men and women. Each of them was learning to map the woods, and this helped them move through fights faster. In fact, they began following the fourth bliss skill: instead of trying to avoid fights, they moved into them as soon as an unmet yearning surfaced. This led to less intense fights that they resolved quickly. Deeper understanding and closeness resulted. They were well on their way to the later phases of true change and dedication to venturing into the scary parts of themselves and their relationship. They still thought of the fairy-tale life but resisted the journeys into the woods less and less, and became closer and closer.

My Fairy Tales, False Beliefs, and Mythology   What myths have you believed about relationships? Are there fairy tales that you secretly hope for despite knowing they are false? Were there family stories or movies that you wish were your reality?

A Thousand Other Self-Deceptions, Smaller but No Less Serious Misconceptions

It's not just the happily-ever-after mythology of white horses and Prince Charming that leads us astray. Numerous misconceptions derail us in our conflict and lead us to settle for less in our relationships. Like the myth of happily ever after, these misconceptions create unrealistic or even harmful relationship expectations and keep us from learning battling to bliss skills. They can cause us to shy away from conflict or lead to covert conflicts and open fights—fights that can never truly be resolved because they are triggered from mistaken beliefs about what constitutes a good relationship.

You will learn to recognize that your fights are rarely about the topic you are fighting about. You must first debunk the misconceptions before you can figure out what the real issues are and engage in productive, growthful battles. To that end, let's examine the most common misconceptions and how to be aware if they are influencing your behavior within a relationship.

Misconception #1: If only I had a relationship, then I'd be happy.

Current relationship studies explode the beliefs that relationships bring lasting happiness and are a panacea for all that ails us. While relationships may boost happiness for a short time, they do not lead to long-term fulfillment and intimacy. In fact, after two years of marriage, the degree of happiness a couple experiences returns to the level of happiness they had individually before they got together (Lucas et al. 2003). It appears we have a happiness set point, and after a period of time, we return to it (Gilbert 2007). Relationships don't make us happy; having a loved one doesn't make us happy—we alone have the power to change our level of happiness. Expecting our partner to change our degree of happiness is unrealistic and a setup for disappointment. When we have magical thinking, we expect too much of relationships. As a result, we often think we made a mistake when the inevitable conflicts arise. If we believe that the relationship is supposed to make us happy, the two-year period of elevated happiness sets us up for a fall when we return to our happiness set point.

Misconception #2: Love means you love and accept me for who I am.

"You should love me just the way I am." Yeah, maybe, but that's not enough. This misconception fosters static, circular relationships. Science reveals that it's more important to love who we are becoming and who we are becoming together. Obviously we need to appreciate who our partner currently is, but what makes for great relationships is supporting him as he becomes his ideal self, who he would be if he fulfilled his dreams.

Relationship research shows that helping others become their best selves and reach their ideal creates the most satisfying relationships, and the more your relationship results in you learning new things and becoming a better person, the better. The more self-expansion people experience from their partner—whether through new ideas, different ways of being, novel experiences, traits, perspectives, knowledge, and so forth—the more satisfied and committed they are in the relationship (Aron et al. 2013).

The goal isn't just to help someone change but to support this person in her efforts to become whom she wants to become. Rusbult, Finkel, and Kumashiro (2009) dubbed this the Michelangelo Phenomenon—we sculpt one another, promoting the other's efforts to reach goals. Every time we interact, we can propel our partner toward his ideal self or push him farther away from his ideal—we help make each other better versions of ourselves.

Misconception #3: Finding "the one" or my "soul mate" is the answer.

When the first blush of romantic love fades, you will be devastated to learn that your soul mate is not perfect in every way. A recent survey discovered that 73 percent of Americans believe that they are destined to find their one, true soul mate (Marist Poll 2011). This belief is often accompanied by the conviction that the right relationship just works out, that you will love each other as you are, and that you have a romantic destiny.

The truth? Relationship research (Knee 1998) reveals that believing in a soul mate and looking for your soul mate actually make it more difficult to experience the intimate relationship you seek! Soul mate seekers are justifying unconscious wishful thinking. They are looking for positive emotional reactions—*chemistry* or *compatibility*—which are two other relationship fallacies! They believe that people either click or not. Research reveals that, as a result, soul mate believers are intensely passionate with partners at first, especially when things are compatible. But, when problems arise, as they inevitably do, they think that means they are not "meant" to be with each other, so they don't deal with the problems and often end promising relationships prematurely.

Rather than battling to bliss, they experience more anxiety and are statistically less likely to forgive their partners and to see possibilities of learning and growing together (Finkel, Burnette, and Scissors 2007). They are more likely to give up when a relationship isn't perfect and start searching again for the "right" match, or resign themselves to unhappiness. This approach tends to lead to a number of intense but short romances and one-night stands, but not long-term, satisfying relationships.

On the other hand, people who believe in cultivating relationships look for someone who will learn and grow with them, resolve conflicts as they arise, and work on themselves and the relationship. They believe that relationships evolve, grow, and deepen with hard work, even in difficult times and situations. They may be less passionate and satisfied with partners at first compared to soul mate searchers, and they may not have that same euphoric beginning. In fact they are more likely to fight at first, but they have longer and more satisfying relationships over time. They are motivated to solve problems as they arise, are committed to their partner, and evolve and grow together.

Misconception #4: Compatibility matters.

The compatibility misconception—that having a lot in common is a sign that you are "meant" to be together—is a variation on the soul mate misconception. A quick look at dating sites reveals that most singles are advertising for people who share the same interests, who like the same things, and have things in common, thinking that these enhance compatibility and likely will reveal or help them find "the one."

The truth? Compatibility is overrated, according to a number of respected marriage researchers (Marano and Flora 2004), and over-focusing on compatibility can be a sign of trouble. Happy couples are no more or less compatible than unhappy couples. But if one spouse or the other starts to complain, saying, "We're not compatible," or expressing how important compatibility is, what he or she really saying is, "We're not getting along." Compatibility is transient; it comes and goes, and no couple is compatible all the time. Good relationships aren't about being compatible. Couples in blissful relationships work with their differences—and grow from them. What is more important is that they share deeper values, meaning, purpose, and a dedication to growing. What matters are common values, not common interests.

Misconception #5: Chemistry is what counts.

Aaah…romance…flowers…candlelight…dancing under the moon…if there's romance and passion, then there's chemistry and true love. Actually romance and chemistry have very little to do with true love. This misconception is so widespread that even the dictionary gets it wrong, describing romance as: *a) a love affair, especially a brief and intense one; b) sexual love, especially when the other person or the relationship is idealized.* Yikes! Neither one of these is a definition of "true love"—a brief and intense love affair and sexual love where the person or relationship is idealized, but not real!

Romantic moments are great, but basing a relationship on romance is problematic. Solely based on romance, relationships are fragile and one-dimensional. Consider two sets of quotes about chemistry, the first where it exists, the second where it is lost:

"I am so turned on!" "She drives me crazy—I can't think of anything else." "I'm falling in love—it hit me like a ton of bricks." "We're madly in love."

and

"I'm not turned on by him anymore." "We just don't have chemistry." "We've fallen out of love."

While there is some truth to chemistry, relying on it as *the* relationship measure can cause huge problems. First, when the chemistry is great, couples often fail to have meaningful or combative discussions about what really matters to them—they are so turned on that they are relating with their bodies and not their minds. Second, when the chemistry weakens as it invariably does, couples become upset and fight about the wrong things—why the chemistry is gone from the relationship. As a result, they may end a potentially deep and intimate relationship prematurely.

In reality, chemistry involves experiencing a chemical rush. People newly in love and in the throes of romantic love experience a surge of chemicals—hormones, serotonin, and dopamine. Love is an emotional, chemical, and physical experience. If you do a brain scan of people as they look at a photo of their romantic interest, their brains look like somebody with obsessive compulsion disorder or someone with a drug problem (Marazziti et al. 1999). This explains the obsessive nature of early romantic love, what we call falling in love, where it's hard to concentrate on daily activities. Professor Helen Fisher (2004), a Rutgers anthropologist, discovered that people who are newly infatuated (notice we didn't say "in love") spend as much as 85 percent of their day thinking about the object of their passion. They're high, obsessed, and in an altered state, which explains those "lovesick" feelings we sometimes have. It's a brief chemical experience. These chemical reactions don't last, and while exciting, they aren't the stuff of long lasting, satisfying intimacy.

Many people think that when the chemical reaction runs its course, that they have "fallen out of love." Not necessarily. They may be getting ready for the next phase of love, often called companionate love (Sternberg 1986). Companionate love, as opposed to the throes of early infatuation, or passionate love, is a less intense but tremendously powerful combination of attachment, intimacy, commitment, and deep affection, which then can evolve to consummate love, a sense of bliss.

Misconception #6: Attraction means it's right.

"Not my type; I can't be with someone I'm not attracted to," or "I'm not that attracted to you." Not being attracted may not be problematic. Attraction is just as likely to lead to hell as heaven. Who we are attracted to isn't necessarily who is best for us and in fact, is often the opposite. It's an automatic response to people who unconsciously represent aspects of our relationship with our parents. The stronger the attraction, the more they represent either that quality itself or its mirror image; a distant father leads to you being attracted to unavailable men, or an abusive father leads you to be attracted to milquetoast men. In fact, people we aren't all that attracted to might just be better partners for us.

We form an unconscious pattern of what love looks and "feels like" from our early relationship with our parents—what scientists call our "attachment schema" (Siegel 2012a). This becomes our template for relationships and determines to whom we are attracted as adults. We wouldn't see it as "love" unless it "felt" like what we experienced as love in early childhood, no matter how bad it may have been in the first place. In simplified terms, if either or both of our parents were distant, we will equate love with distance. If they were abusive, dismissive, or overprotective, we will associate those qualities with love and be attracted to people who "feel" the same way to us. Unconsciously, we are seeking to complete or repair our early childhood patterns (Hendrix 2007).

Inevitably, the old patterns from your childhood will surface, and you'll stop being attracted. That doesn't mean you've fallen out of love or picked the wrong person; it means that it's time to work your deeper issues that drew you to this person in the first place.

Misconception #7: All you need is love.

Naïve, simplistic formulas like this one are dead ends. Love is *not* enough. Relationships, like any growing, organic thing, require maintenance and nurturing to grow. Great relationships don't just "happen"—they take skill, practice, and dedication to learning and growing, not just love.

This misconception makes people lazy in love. They fail to take responsibility for growing the relationship, which includes having difficult and, at times, disturbing conversations. They invest love with a magical power that absolves them of having to doing anything but exist in a fake-blissful state. At the extreme, we ignore our partner's drinking problem because this belief leads people to think they should also accept the other totally. It also leads to avoidance of conflict. The avoided issues build up and unhappiness builds to ineffective explosions and, at the extreme, divorce.

Investment and skill form basic elements of the blissful relationship equation. Yet many of us assume that love is supposed to be easy. We think just because we are in relationships that we know how to navigate them. When it gets hard, we believe that something is wrong, rather than looking to develop the skill to deal with the challenges. We say things like, "It isn't right. It's too much work." Sure, love helps, but it's not sufficient. We need to work at it too.

We don't expect other aspects of our life to be easy or just come naturally, which is why we work on perfecting our golf swing, get training to enhance our professional skill, or attend yoga classes. Yet, when we believe that love is all we need, we don't invest in our relationships or continue to learn, grow, and develop. We are more likely to invest our time and money to study martial arts than marital arts.

True Romance

Letting go of myths and fairy tales doesn't mean you let go of romance. You can still have the romance—you should have it. To enjoy true romance, though, consider an alternative definition for it: *a spirit or feeling of adventure, excitement, and the potential for heroic achievement.* It is about going into the unknown, Sondheim's woods, with the potential for heroism. This means developing the skills that take us into the woods where we can engage in the battle, clear-eyed and fighting off the enemy of true romance—a lack of awareness of your own deepest needs and those of your partner. It's scary to surface childhood traumas or to confront your mate on a sensitive subject, but this is the way to bliss. Once you move beyond myths and misconceptions, tough truths are still hard to take, but you face them courageously knowing that doing so will help you grow and become more and more real, present, and authentic—you take the heroic steps of facing and sharing all of yourself, including your tears, fears, joys, gifts, weaknesses, and truths.

It's easy to buy chocolates and flowers or make reservations for dinner at a romantic restaurant, but it's much harder to share your reservations about yourself, your partner, the relationship—harder, but far more beneficial for a meaningful, long-term union. So jettison those myths and misconceptions and move on to this more difficult but more rewarding heroic reality.

Taking this step will allow you to tap into your deepest hungers and ultimately find your way through the woods with even deeper meaning and purpose. The compass to guide you on your journey will be your deepest *yearnings*—the subject of our next chapter.

PART 2

The Art of the Fight

Six Skills for Battling to Bliss

CHAPTER 4

Yearn

Discover and Follow Your Yearning

Why do we fight? Because we *yearn*.

No, we don't yearn for the clothes to be picked up, for the cap to be put back on the toothpaste, for the toilet seat to be up or down, or for the garbage to be taken out, or even for sex. We yearn for what these actions represent—what they mean to us deep inside. We yearn to be seen and heard, to love and be loved, to express ourselves, to make a difference, or to be part of something greater than ourselves. We yearn all the time, though we rarely recognize it. These yearnings are powerful currents running beneath the surface, and though we might not be conscious of them, they exert an influence on our behavior—they propel us to love and compel us to fight.

Finding and following your yearnings is the first bliss skill. Unmet yearnings are at the heart of every fight, and when they are met, they become the heart of our intimacy and satisfaction. Learn to unpack your fights to get to the yearning underneath. Actively pursue your yearning moment to moment, and you have set a solid cornerstone for intimacy.

Yearning is no soft, needy, touchy-feely, nice-if-you-like-that sort of thing. Each of us—all seven billion people on the planet—has been hardwired to yearn. Harness the power of yearning or you'll be negating one of the things that brings you the most satisfaction and the most power to your relationships.

Nothing wondrous has been achieved except by yearning—the yearning to love, to connect, to create, to aspire to mastery, to matter, to make a difference. Yearning, when properly channeled, not only brings you love, satisfaction, intimacy, and closeness, but also makes you your best and an even bigger contribution to your relationship and your world. It is yearning that sparks the creation of everything from inspiring art, soul-stirring music, majestic cathedrals, and cures for diseases to great love and service. Unacknowledged, unchanneled, and unmet yearning makes you empty, unhappy, unsatisfied, and miserable in your relationship and your life. Unmet yearnings erupt in your fights in a misguided attempt to get them met. Yearnings addressed, channeled, and satisfied bring intimacy, bliss, and contribution.

Our yearnings spur us to relate, support, care, matter, make a difference, and go for greatness. And because we are designed to yearn, when they aren't met, we are designed to be upset—*really* upset—to get our attention and get us back on track. We're supposed to protest, object, and feel distress when we aren't fulfilling our yearning; we're supposed to feel empty and cranky and angry enough to do something about it. And you thought you were just having a fight over who takes the trash out.

Do You Yearn?

How do you know if you have yearnings? Well, if you are breathing, you are yearning. Unmet yearnings surface in many ways; as vague dissatisfactions, undefined longings, stagnant ruts, relationship problems, or out-and-out fights (Wright and Wright 2013). Operating beneath our conscious awareness, these yearnings draw us to enter into and engage in relationships. They are also the fuel that drives fights. In fact, fighting with your lover is one of the ways you can address your unmet yearnings by bringing them to the surface.

Take a look at these scenarios of yearnings unmet. Which one do you relate to most?

- You have the same fights over and over again—that never seem to go anywhere.

- You are vaguely dissatisfied in your relationship, but can't quite put your finger on it. You're not being beaten, he isn't having an affair, he's not an alcoholic, so what's the problem?

- The honeymoon feeling is gone. Things are decent in your relationship, and you want more, but you don't want anything to rock the boat.

- You're having a normal conversation and all of a sudden, BAM! One or the other of you is triggered seemingly out of nowhere, and an awful fight erupts. Things are tense, and you know that if you could just go on a vacation or have more sex, then everything would be okay.

- You are afraid to bring up problems, so you don't, or you bring up a problem in your relationship, something you want different, a preference, and your partner stonewalls, complains back, or walks away.

These scenarios are all examples of your yearnings *not* being met. Your yearnings are like an inner GPS, pointing you in a direction of more satisfaction. When you are using this skill and actively pursuing your yearning to be seen, heard, valued, loved; to matter; to make a difference, you mine your fights to realize what you truly are yearning for. You look beneath your dissatisfaction, the surface tension, the ruts and routines to discover what you yearn for. You ask for what you need directly, resolve your fights by getting to the yearning at the heart of the fight, and develop more closeness by sharing your deep yearnings with your partner.

Sense the difference in these scenarios where yearnings are satisfied from the ones you considered earlier:

- Your partner's face lights up when he sees you.

- You're upset and call your partner for support, and she is there for you.

- You express your dissatisfaction and ask directly for what you desire.

- You celebrate each other's successes.

When you successfully apply this skill, you feel the satisfaction of meeting your yearnings to express and be valued, to be cared about, seen, heard, and appreciated.

What Are Yearnings, and What Do We Yearn For?

Yearnings are powerful, deeply engrained, evolutionary adaptive mechanisms that initially developed for our survival. They drive us to relate, to bond, and to commune with others, as well as to develop ourselves. And when your yearnings aren't met, they trigger the alarms that commonly lead to fights.

How do you know what you yearn for? Wants are specific and require a close match—your partner needs to do what you say. Yearnings are much larger, are more general, and can be addressed in an infinite number of ways. Just knowing what you yearn for starts to meet your deeper yearning. For example, by knowing that you yearn to be seen, you are paying attention to yourself and what is going on deep inside you. This knowledge is calming and satisfying in itself, and it's something you can do without involving your partner.

Identify Your Yearnings   Use this chart to help you learn the language of yearning. Read through the list. Best, say the words out loud to see which ones resonate with you. Chances are they all will, but some may hit you more than others. When you are fighting, use the list to identify what you really yearn for underneath the fight. Get used to applying this skill and name your yearnings as often as you can.

UNIVERSAL YEARNINGS

I yearn...

To be secure
- to exist
- to be safe, to be secure
- to connect, to bond
- to trust

To love & care for, respond to others
- to care for
- to nurture
- to love

To relate, see and be seen, know and be known, connect
- to be seen, heard, known, understood
- to see, hear, & know others
- to touch & be touched
- to feel "felt"
- to empathize

To have my existence appreciated
- to love & be loved
- to be affirmed, appreciated
- to be cared for
- to be respected

To express my essence, sense of self, potential
- to express
- to experience fully
- to learn, grow, develop
- to create
- to be separate, to have an identity

- to influence
- to excel
- to fulfill my potential

To have a sense of mattering
- to matter
- to be valued and to value
- to contribute
- to do what I came here on Earth to do
- to make a difference
- to please God
- to fulfill my purpose
- to unfold my destiny

To be connected with others
- to belong
- to connect
- to matter
- to be close
- to communicate with others
- to commune with others
- to make deep contact with another
- to be intimate

To connect to something greater
- to be connected to something greater than myself
- to feel connected to the greater whole
- to be one with all
- to know God or the creator
- for union with all that is

Make Love *and* War

Intimacy isn't child's play. We know that fighting with someone you love may seem counterintuitive, but it's not when you consider that the forces that lead us to get into relationships and guide us through the woods are the same forces that, when threatened, lead us to fight, distance, separate, or hold back. If you care deeply about your spouse or partner, why do you speak harshly or engage in verbal battles? The answer is that you are driven by a powerful motive: you want to connect, and you want to connect to fulfill your yearning.

Most fighting is an attempt to fulfill a yearning. Unfortunately, we are usually unaware of that yearning, so we fight about the wrong things. Fulfilling your yearnings can help you and your partner analyze fights, increasing the odds that you'll change your behavior—be on time, clean the house, put the toilet seat down, and achieve other tangible results. More importantly, fulfilling your yearnings leads to learning, growing, and developing, not to mention joy and even bliss for each of you. And when your yearnings aren't fulfilled—when the person you love sends a signal that you don't matter or aren't being heard—then resentment builds and fights erupt.

The concept of yearning emerged from our study of people who live great lives characterized by satisfying relationships, fulfilling careers, service, and higher purpose. They accomplished impressive goals and lifestyles by tending to their inner yearnings, not just to external outcomes (Wright and Wright 2013). These high performers had no patience for unnecessary, unsatisfying, and unfulfilling behavior and activities. They dug deeper to see what it is that they truly yearn for and then admitted it and pursued it directly.

Before I married Judith, I had already done a lot of personal development work to move beyond being like my taciturn father and controlling mother, which proved to be insufficient when Judith went into our You're Just Like Your Mother/Father fight. My parents were great partners, but my mother complained that my father was friendly to others, but too emotionally distant with her until a massive stroke made him very emotionally uncensored and flowing, like a two-year-old. So it was a huge surprise to me when Judith began complaining that I was just like my father *and* my mother—controlling and punishing in my silence.

Judith yearned to be seen, to be valued for who she was, not for her compliance to my systems from kitchen organization to how much flame was under the pots and pans. She felt hurt, insignificant, and frustrated at my control. Our conflict invariably ended in Judith complaining that I was just like my mother or my father depending on my particular way of being. At first, I rejected her complaints as wanton attacks, but over time I realized that not only were her yearnings to be seen and to be affirmed not being met but I was missing out on my deeper yearnings to be close and affirmed, myself.

The breakthrough in these logjams happened when a spiritual teacher of mine berated me for my control and told me to leave Judith alone and learn to enjoy the ride. To my amazement, we began enjoying ourselves more, things became more relaxed, and I was able to see that the yearning behind my control was really for more contact that could only be realized if I relaxed my control. Surprisingly, Judith ended up coming around on the things I wanted too, when her yearning to be seen and to matter was being met.

I was then able to better recognize my parents' unmet yearnings that had gone into their lifestyle—from a background of chaos and physical conflict on my dad's side and of profound cruelty on my mother's. They yearned for basic safety, which resulted in my mom's control and my father's distance to protect us from his anger. Building on their foundation, I was able to fulfill more advanced yearnings for contact, affirmation, and growing together in even more fulfilling ways. As it turned out, I was like both of them on the surface as well as like them in deeper yearning, only I was able to build on their foundation and meet even more yearnings than they had been able to meet.

Like many couples, we got in fights because we did not know a better way to meet our yearnings. (We still do when we need to find better ways to do things.) Failing to understand what we yearned for, we felt upset, irritated, angry, or even despairing, often at seemingly inconsequential things. We wanted something to change or to be different. We would fight for what we wanted and miss the yearning underneath.

I took years to grasp that I was fighting with Bob as a way to be seen, heard, and understood. Early on, my assertiveness was nonverbal, existing largely in my journal entries and the thoughts that coursed through my head. Highly assertive, Bob would fire out his points like bullets from a machine gun. Over time I began to call time-outs during our disagreements just to collect my thoughts and recognize my deeper feelings—my yearning. Gradually I learned how to engage in the moment of conflict and articulate what I needed from Bob. Through the demanding, yelling, and the hurt feelings, we integrated our yearnings into our arguments and developed greater empathy for ourselves and each other.

Yearning vs. Wanting

Bob was yearning for order and safety along with being seen and affirmed. He was trying to get it by wanting things done his way. Fights get circular when we only say what we want instead of what we yearn for. Like Bob, too often we just complain or try to force our will, but even when we ask sweetly for what we want, it is rarely a request grounded in yearning. Psychologists and economic researchers call this *miswanting*: wanting something that we mistakenly think will make us happy (Wilson and Gilbert 2000). We are all "poor affective forecasters"—meaning that we pretty much suck at predicting what will make us happy, and even predicting what will make us unhappy (Wilson and Gilbert 2005).

Yet these mistaken wants are most often what we fight about. We want our partner to sit up straight, balance the checkbook, stop being stupid, treat us a particular way, pick the kids up from school without complaint. And while these are worthy desires, often we "want" them in order to avoid the upset, to make the bad feelings go away, or to win the fight. Without being aware of yearning and focusing our fights on it, we can get what we want and still be unsatisfied.

Think about a relationship conflict in which you convinced your partner to concede you were right or to do what you wanted, but you didn't feel either vindicated or happy about it. Yes, he now remembers to put down the toilet seat, but you still don't feel loved or affirmed. She might consent to more sex, but you still don't feel valued and wanted. The deeper yearning remains untouched, and so your fight exists on the surface of things—you'll never reach bliss this way. True satisfaction, intimacy, and fulfillment come from understanding why your wants matter to you.

The Neuroscience of Yearning

Why is meeting our yearning so much more satisfying than getting what we want? One reason neuroscience researchers have found is that wanting and yearning activate different centers of the brain, each leading to different results—one that's satisfying and one that's not. As you learn the bliss skills, you will be learning to live more in the yearning center. But first, understand the challenges with wanting.

Wanting activates the pleasure center of the brain called our wanting center (Berridge 2009) or excitatory center (Doidge 2007). This center is fueled by dopamine—it gets us high. While this motivates us to pursue our desires, the high is a short-lived, temporary "fix" that doesn't satisfy or fulfill us. And when the temporary high fades, it triggers yet another "want" to get that dopamine squirt, an addictive cycle that can never bring us true satisfaction. Yearning, on the other hand, activates the pleasure center neuroscientists refer to as our satisfaction center (Doidge 2007) or liking center (Berridge 2009) and we call the seat of our yearning. This pleasure center of our brain is fueled by the opioid neurotransmitters, which are responsible for deep contentment. When we meet our yearnings in our relationship—when we connect with our yearning to love and be loved; to be seen, heard, and touched; to matter; to connect—we activate this pleasure center and experience true satisfaction. Like strengthening a muscle with exercise and progressively heavier weights, you are learning to activate this center better.

Keeping this scientific divide between wanting and yearning in mind makes a big difference in how you fight and what you get out of your conflicts. We don't *yearn* to win a fight; we *want* to win a fight, which can give you a dopamine high but also leaves you high…and dry. You might feel smug and superior for a moment, but not close, if it doesn't meet your yearning. Going deeper and discovering what you yearn for is what brings satisfaction.

Analyzing relationship battles this way helps you look for the yearning beneath your miswanting. Many times you don't know what you really need in life or from a relationship. You may believe that you really must have more sex, a large salary, a plum job, an exotic vacation, or even a clean house. If you're conscious that you yearn for more than this, relationship battles can be an intimate forum for illuminating these deeper desires.

Consider George and Rita. George fought for a neat house, and Rita resisted—their version of the Up and Down Toilet Seats and Other Domestic Disputes. She felt invalidated by his demands. For years, the battle raged until George revealed that having things out of place brought the upsets of his childhood into the present. As the first-born son of a chaotic home and a dissolving parental union, George was a good boy "holding his breath" to hold the family together. George yearned for security, and a well-ordered house was his way of satisfying this deeper need.

Once George became aware that he wanted more than proper places for books and silverware—that his arguments with Rita were about deeper issues rooted in his childhood—he found more solace in Rita's steadfast devotion. Their conflicts became richer, more intimate activities, and the house came into better order, from silverware to books, to their sons' rooms, and more. They were using their bliss skills and getting to the heart of the fight.

George's understanding of his yearning softened him, and he relaxed more. It rendered him more open to Rita's struggle to keeping a tidy house. She was finally able to communicate that she felt hurt that George seemed to care more about a clean house than about her. Through their arguments, she came to realize that she resented George wanting a dollhouse (with her as the doll) instead of a home with her.

As they sought to identify the yearning beneath the wants, George discovered not only his yearning for the security that a neat house represented, but also his desire to know he mattered to Rita. Rita also hungered to matter, and each of them yearned to be seen and known. When George acknowledged his insecurity caused by a disorderly house, Rita was able to recognize her yearning to be loved for who she was, not for how she looked or what she did. Understanding each other's deeper yearnings motivated them to cooperate and have a house and relationship they were both proud of.

Verbal fights can surface this deeper yearning, but decoding the yearning takes time, persistence, and the process you are learning throughout this book. For now, though, recognize that your fighting has a purpose beyond the mundane and the superficial, and the purpose is powerful—to fulfill your yearning. The more you understand about yearning, the easier it will be to make your relationship battles and other times more intimate and meaningful.

What ticks couples off?	What makes couples tick?
Not meeting their yearnings	Meeting their yearnings
The fear of not getting them met	

What Makes Couples Tick and What Ticks Couples Off

When you think about the good times in your relationship, chances are you attribute them to circumstances or behaviors: the fun you had, the romantic dinner, the long walk along the lake, the great sex, the way he was so nice or she was so sexy. You don't equate the good times with "Oh, our yearnings were met." And, when you think about your fights, your thoughts may revolve around your partner's dastardly ways and recurring themes—the money fight (or what we refer to as Dueling Over Dollars) or "We always go to your mother's for holidays" (Family Feuds), or "Why did you have to say that?" (You Embarrassed Me). You don't immediately consider the unmet yearning that exists beneath the surface or your fear of never satisfying this yearning. Failing to understand these powerful forces operating underneath the good times and the bad means you won't respect their power or harness them effectively for great fights and great relationships.

We Are Designed to Yearn

We are *designed* to yearn. Our yearning to connect and be cared for isn't just an emotional preference; it's a biological need paramount to our survival (Lieberman 2013). Yearning to bond and to love ensures that parents take care of their children. Our yearning to exist, connect, empathize, and commune with others increases our chances for survival and thriving by forming groups, sharing resources, and enhancing protection and fending off enemies.

We've been programmed by evolution to be rewarded when we follow our yearning. When our yearnings are met, our system is flooded with feel-good neurochemicals (Coan 2008). We feel good, really good—satisfied, fulfilled, delighted, full of goodwill, even blissful! But when these systems are threatened in any way—when our yearnings aren't met, our partner is distancing or unavailable, or the relationship feels threatened—KABOOM! It triggers a neurobiological alarm in response to threatened loss or separation, flooding us with feel-bad stress hormones and neurochemicals, spiking our arousal system and sparking us to fight, flight, or flee (Panksepp 1998).

In the heat of an argument, you assume that your anger, fear, and sadness are because of your partner's behavior, the subject you are fighting about, or the situation. While you may indeed be hurt and pissed that he's acting like a jerk, the intensity of your emotions has a more primal source in this basic neurochemistry.

Lifelong Yearning

Yearnings are continually activated throughout our lifetime. Yearning for love, connection, and security starts with your attachment to your caregivers as an infant and continues throughout adulthood into your romantic relationships. We all have a fundamental need for connection and a profound fear of losing it (Bowlby 1969). Underneath all of our interactions with our loved ones are attachment-related yearnings to be connected, to be secure, to be comforted and protected (Bowlby 1988).

See if you can relate to these hardwired relationship drivers—the four aspects of our attachment system that define our relationships as children and our adult love relationships:

- for us to *seek proximity* with our caregiver as a child and with our loved one as an adult

- to rely on our caregiver or partner for a *safe haven* for comfort and support when we feel frightened, threatened, or in danger

- for our caregiver or partner to provide a *secure base* for us to learn, grow, and explore

- to protest when we experience *separation distress* when our caregiver or partner isn't available, responsive, or engaged with us

We know you're a grown-up now and no longer running to Mom's skirts for security, but these dynamics continue to be the foundations for adult romantic attachment and intimacy.

When we experience support, closeness, and security with our partner, and our yearnings are met, we feel great. But when we don't—when relationship fights or life stresses threaten our safe haven—we experience attachment alarm and primal panic as the fear of danger or loss of our loved one (Bowlby 1973). This unconscious alarm or panic triggers our fights. How we respond to this panic is often at the root of our conflict. It can ignite or exacerbate the fight. For example, each of the following fights and levels of unhappiness in relationship is rooted in attachment alarm or panic:

- *Why can't you come home sooner?* We seek proximity and a safe haven. We yearn to matter and be secure.

- *Why don't we have sex more?* We yearn to be comforted and feel safe. We seek proximity and connection.

- *You don't love me like you used to.* We seek a secure base. We yearn to feel secure and to matter.

- *Why are you so distant, pulling away, leaving…?* We seek connection and a secure base. We yearn to connect.

Corresponding to our attachment system is our innate caregiving system, the evolutionary foundation of our yearning to love, care for, nurture, and protect another (Bowlby 1969). While attachment and caregiving systems allow us to feel solid, secure, and cared for, another system, the intersubjectivity system, provides the foundation for empathy. It promotes our capacities to see, feel, and know each other—to sense what is on our partner's mind and heart, to understand how he or she thinks, feels, and experiences life (Stern 2004). It helps us experience warmth and deep intimacy with our partner, to see and be seen, to commune, to "feel felt" (Siegel 2012b) by another. While attachment provides security and protection, intersubjectivity allows us to communicate and facilitates our understanding. It is this ability that allowed us to develop intuitive understanding of others that helped us survive (Blakeslee 2006).

Many fights stem from our yearning to be known and appreciated—the yearning to connect, to know and be known, to understand, and be understood. Fighting is often an attempt to establish this important connection: "You never listen to me. I *told* you I had an important presentation today. Talking to you is like talking to a post. You don't even see me!"

These evolutionary systems continue to be triggered and can develop throughout our lives—from the yearning of a two-year-old to be separate, to express his or her will, and to have influence; to an adolescent yearning to belong while at the same time to express individuality; to a young adult's yearning to excel, to master, to become a unique individual; to the yearning of adulthood to grow and transform, to make one's mark, to experience life fully; to the yearning of mature adulthood to feel universal belonging and mastery of ourselves (Wright and Wright 2012).

Childhood Yearnings Triggered in Romantic Relationships

Your patterns in your relationships have underlying roots in childhood—whether you've continually chosen commitment-phobes, unavailable objects of desire, or clingy or possessive partners. Your childhood attachment style becomes an "internal working model" for relationships (Bowlby 1973) that determines who you are attracted to, who you are with, and how you relate. Whatever felt like love in your early years becomes your template for love in your adult life. If your father was distant, for example, you'll unconsciously seek love with and pick unavailable men, or you'll seek his mirror image and may choose someone who is clingy but equally unavailable for adult partnership. The same pains, hurts, and fears you experienced in childhood will surface again in your adult romantic relationships—and will trigger some of your most painful fights. Yet, when you can recognize your true yearnings underneath your fights and practice the other bliss skills, you can not only heal some of the childhood hurts, but also forge a new intimacy with your partner.

Jacky picked an unresponsive guy just like her father. Available guys seemed weak to her and didn't turn her on. But now those unmet childhood yearnings erupted anew in fights like: "I might as well have stayed single for all the attention I get from you. It's like trying to talk to a stone. You're as bad as my father, never paying attention, always rejecting me. I can't stand it!" Her yearning to be seen, to be heard, to connect, to matter, to be cared about is emerging in the fight. As she learns to identify her yearnings and work to get them met, rather than just be frustrated and harangue her partner, she can begin to heal her childhood pain and to develop a closer relationship with her partner.

We feel safe, confident, and secure when our partner or attachment figure is nearby, available, and responsive to us. When we feel a threat to the relationship or to ourselves, we become anxious and seek the support and attention of our partner or others. Ideally, our loved ones serve as our safe haven during these times. And if not, fighting is likely.

For example, Jacky and Jeff's relationship was a mystery to their friends. One minute they were lovey-dovey and affirming, and then Jacky was yelling at Jeff. Her reaction seemed incomprehensible unless you knew that there were times when Jeff would withdraw and that his withdrawal would trigger an attachment alarm in Jacky. Initially, sensing his distance, she would respond by getting agitated and aggressive. Sensing her alarm, he would flee. The more agitated Jacky got, the more Jeff pulled away until Jacky was in full primal panic at being abandoned and he was in full primal panic at her anger. They would cool off, and each would seek reassurance from the other to reestablish the secure attachment, to know the other was there for them. It was not until they understood these triggering events that they were able to begin managing these situations and experiencing the deeper intimacy of understanding and tending to each other.

Learn to Yearn

With practice you will develop the skill of yearning as Jacky and Jeff did. One of the best ways to learn about your yearnings is when they are not being met and erupt in problems and fights. But in the heat of a fight, it's often difficult to go deep inside to discover your unmet yearning. Don't give up. You can always dig in to find the unmet yearning *after* the fight. When the dust starts to settle, ask yourself: *What was that all about? What was I yearning for underneath? What did I really want?* Recall the list of yearnings. Did you want to feel safe and secure? Did you want to be seen, heard, affirmed? To know that you matter? To feel connected? To feel potent? Always choose the most basic of the yearnings and talk about them. Make sure you both are recognizing your yearning just as Jeff recognized his yearning for security and Jacky recognized her yearning for affirmation.

Post-Fight Reflection   Revved up in a fight, you may not be able to find the space and distance to ask yourself—and answer—*What is really going on? What am I yearning for?* Look for what you yearn for *after* the heat of the fight has cooled, your rational self is back on line, and you can think and feel more accurately and clearly. Use the chart of yearnings and pick the ones that describe what you longed for most in the fight. Now, share that with your partner.

Sometimes even after the fight, it is difficult to decode the content of the fight directly. In that case, reflect on your fight and ask yourself: *What did I want? What was I trying to get across? What did I want to happen?* Digging beneath wants to the deeper yearning is a skill. If you ask yourself, "I wanted X so that Y," about each want in the fight, you will discover more wants. Keep adding "I wanted Y so that Z" to your discovery. You will be digging beneath wants to yearnings.

Here are some examples:

I wanted him to know what an idiot he was being so that he never does that again …
> …so that I don't have to feel that horrible again
> …so that I can feel good
> …so that I can feel special and loved

Means: I yearn to be loved and to matter.

I wanted to punish him for being so mean to me…
> …so that he can feel as bad as I do
> …so that he'll know what it's like
> …so that he'll know how I feel
> …so that he understands me and doesn't hurt me

Means: I yearn to be seen, understood, known, protected.

I wanted her to back off and stop nagging ...

    ...so that she stops yanking my chain

    ...so that she's not always putting me down and indicting me

    ...so that she starts appreciating me and all the stuff I do

    ...so that she treats me like I'm special, not a piece of dirt

    ...so that I know she respects me

    ...so that she appreciates me

Means: I yearn to be affirmed, appreciated, respected.

I wanted her to pick up her stuff and stop making such a trash pile of our house

    ...so that we have a clean house

    ...so that I don't trip over her shit

    ...so that I can come home to a nice house

    ...so that after I work all day, it's nice to come home

    ...so that I'm not so upset when I walk in the door

    ...so that I don't have to feel like I live in a crazy mess like my old man

    ...so that things aren't so chaotic

    ...so that I feel calm and safe, like crazy things aren't going to happen

Means: I yearn to feel secure.

Use the "So That" Test to Find Your Yearnings   Write down what you wanted in your fight—even if it was irresponsible, outrageous, indignant, or petulant. What did you want to happen? What result did you hope for? Now, dig beneath, using the "I wanted X so that Y" format. Use the examples above to guide you. Keep adding "so that" to whatever was going on until you get to the deeper yearning. Not sure you're there yet? Check the yearnings chart to see if what you came up with is close to something on the list. Still not sure? When you finally get to a sense of *Ahhh, that's it*, feel more calm and grounded, and there's nothing much more to say, you've discovered your yearning. Now share this with your partner.

After the "so that" exercise reveals the yearning, tell your partner what you really yearned for rather than what you were arguing about and encourage your partner to tell you what he yearned for in that fight too. Don't let too much time pass after your argument before having this conversation. Keep doing this after every fight or upset, and after a while, you'll find yourself catching your yearning sooner or even during the fight. And when you get really good at knowing what your yearnings are, you'll identify and meet them proactively. You will be asking for what you need and want directly, achieving greater intimacy while avoiding some fights!

Once you identify your yearning, you will be much less likely to accelerate interactions because of primal panic or to choose cool withdrawal when you fear your yearning might not be met.

Where Real Relationship Magic Comes From

When we use our fights to develop our yearning and we understand and express what we are truly yearning for, we don't just feel better; we become better. Our loving relationship expands our confidence, our sense of who we are. We send out signals that positively affect hormone levels, cardiovascular function, body rhythms, and the immune system of the other (Graham 2013). We deal with conflict less reactively and more productively. We more easily roll with the inevitable hurts of relationships—and when we get mad at our partner, we aren't as belligerent (Gouin et al. 2010).

When our yearnings are met and we feel safe and secure, it's empowering. We are more flexible in our thinking and more open to challenging our beliefs. Ironically, the more we are able to reach out to our partners and get our needs met, the more independent and separate we can be (Feeney 2007). We're like a young child who, once he catches sight of his mom, feels safe to freely explore his world.

We've all seen people who flourish in careers, make great friends, and feel more satisfied when they're in good relationships, and we've also seen people who struggle when they're in disempowering relationships. In our research (Wright and Wright 2013), we found that people who live great lives are consistently guided by their deeper yearnings. They don't invest much in nonproductive behaviors and activities that provide little long-term satisfaction or meaning. And, when they realize their fights aren't about the fight and dig deeper to see what it is that they truly yearn for, they are able to go into the metaphorical woods and use their bliss skills.

They are battling to bliss and getting to the heart of the conflict with the first skill, yearning, and they are beginning their next steps into the full adventure of life. Their yearning is directing their lives to greater satisfaction, and they are naturally beginning to learn the next skill in the bliss process: *engaging*.

CHAPTER 5

Engage!

The Seven Rules for Fighting Fair and Loving Well

I t isn't sufficient just to yearn, or even to simply express your yearning. You must *engage*—the second bliss skill—and make moves and take risks to meet your yearnings and get to the heart of your fights. True love requires full engagement—going for it in the relationship, fighting to meet your yearnings, being real, risking, and making mistakes as you full-out encounter each other.

True love means that you roll up your sleeves and dig into the relationship. You enter the woods, bump into each other, adjust course, and find your path. You become more spontaneous, less careful, and more your real self—a self you may not have even met yet. Yeah, it's messier (we warned you love is messy), and you'll step on each other's toes, but it's much more fulfilling, exciting, and satisfying. You'll be learning and growing together. Your fighting will pay off, and you'll experience more happiness and well-being, what positive psychology researchers call leading "an engaged life" or being "in the flow" (Seligman 2002, 116–117). Your encounters with your partner become fresh and exciting, which is key to having a satisfying relationship (Tsapelas, Aron, and Orbuch 2009).

Conflict isn't such a big deal when you learn how to engage effectively. You move right through it. If you have a baseline of speaking up, asking for what you want, expressing your anger and resentment, as well as engaging in positive aspects such as affirmation, affection, and humor, conflict is much more natural and much more easily resolved.

What Engaging Is—and What It Is Not

You may think you are engaging—you talk, you do things together, you listen intently to your partner, or you do your fair share of the chores. Or maybe you have frequent, loud and tumultuous fights. When we speak of engaging, however, we mean something more than activity or active listening or active fights. Real, creative engaging happens when you are truly present, addressing your yearning, and are emotionally aware, available, and expressive (Wright and Wright 2013).

It's also more than being active, lively, or energetic. There are plenty of Susie Sunshines in the world who mindlessly chat and act happy to avoid real engagement and couples who do a lot together, from having sex to going on great vacations. To be truly engaged, though, you have to be conscious and in contact with deeper yearnings—your own and those of your partner. It's being real, vulnerable, and truthful.

When you engage, you are forthright and straight, not manipulating, managing, or buttering him up before you talk, or waiting until she's in a good mood. You risk, make mistakes, and even engage in destructive behaviors, but you take responsibility. You engage creatively—learning, growing, and being fascinated with life rather than zoned out from too much Facebook, football, or other frivolous addictive pursuits. Watching too much TV, even if you are doing it together, doesn't qualify as engaging, nor is sharing other soft addictions (Wright 2006)—like when Bob is transfixed by his computer screen and Judith, knowing he's not listening, tells him, "The house is on fire," just to see if he is the slightest bit present.

Engagement is not active listening. In fact, *active listening is some of the worst relationship advice you'll ever get.* True engaging is being real, not careful. Being cautious with one another, using stilted "I messages" of active or reflective listening language such as, "I hear what you are saying," "I feel hurt when you don't let the dog out, and I would prefer you do it," or, "You feel angry because I didn't pick up the cleaning today," doesn't help you get to the heart of the fight. Yes, you should take responsibility, but real couples—happy ones—don't speak this way (Gottman 1994). In intimate relationships, these expressions fail to reveal what is really going on with you and your partner. They don't promote meaningful life changes. In fact, active listening was rated the worst marital intervention—research showed it doesn't work (Hahlweg et al. 1998).

More of Everything from Messy to Magnificent

True intimacy demands that you engage a lot. When you do, you experience more of everything—the good and the bad, the sublime, the maddening, and the magical. Sharing yourself and your life with your partner, you have both destructive and constructive interactions; ones that tear your relationship down or build it up, that threaten intimacy, but ultimately deepen it. Remember, fighting and negativity serve a purpose in relationships—they help to surface unexpressed yearnings, allow you to smooth out interaction patterns that aren't working, and sort through your different perspectives.

We'll give you some ground rules to make the destructive fights and interactions pay off, but for now, know that the point isn't to banish destructive interactions—that's all part of relating—but to cultivate more constructive interactions that override the destructive ones.

Tipping the Balance of Your Relationship

Consider what relationship research has revealed: *Couples don't break up because they are having more fights and nasty, unpleasant interactions— it's because they don't have enough positive ones* (Markman et al. 2010).

Engaging in ways that meet your yearnings and those of your partner tip the balance toward the positive and are critical for relationship success and satisfaction; this is how you'll weather the fights and the down times. Fights look very different against a backdrop of love and affection.

"Just add more positives to your relationship." Sounds easy, right? Simple, maybe, but not easy. Evolution has primed us to look for the negative, so we have to consciously seek the positive, create more pleasant experiences, and soak them in (Hanson 2013). The more we do this, the more resilient we become. We don't get triggered as much by each other's foibles, and we become more open both to ourselves and to our partner's experiences.

The Ratio of Constructive to Destructive

How many more constructive versus destructive interactions do we need? Gottman's research gives us a good guide. In happy couples, the ratio of positive to negative interactions is 5-to-1 in disagreements and fights, and in divorcing couples it's less than one positive (.8) to one negative. And some robust couples, even when fighting, have 20-to-1 positives to negatives (Gottman 2012).

For every destructive move you make, therefore, you need five positives to neutralize the negatives in a fight. That means for every snarky comment, toxic dump, eye roll, contemptuous response, show of disgust, smug shrug, whiney complaint—in essence, for every shitty thing you do—you need five positives to balance it out in a fight. You don't have to keep a tally on a pad of paper, but we're suggesting you be conscious of your positive interactions versus your negative ones. When you're fighting, every time you say, "Good point," instead of "Oh, yeah? Prove it," or laugh at yourself or act curious rather than defensive, you added positives to tip the balance. Your ultimate goal—bliss—requires twenty positives. Even then, you may still do snarky things and blurt caustic comments, but you counterbalance them with many more positive interactions.

The Engagement Continuum: From Neutral-Destructive to Constructive-Creative

Don't make the mistake of trying to eliminate all of your negative interactions. All positive isn't real while too many negatives without enough positives and you're headed to divorce court. Couples interact in a thousand ways that build or tear down a relationship. Many of them are subtle and difficult to assess. Consider a horizontal line along which we arrange interactions from extremely destructive on the left, to profoundly creative and even transformational on the right. The interactions on the left side range from destructive to neutral in the middle with transactions like talking about logistics. While necessary, limiting your interactions to data exchange doesn't move your relationship toward intimacy.

Behaviors on the left side are often automatic and reflexive rather than thoughtful and conscious. While some interactions on the left side can be explosive and even reach cataclysmic proportions, many interactions on the left side are routine, unengaged, surface data exchanges. The content may seem benign, but the interactions can be laced with unconscious hostility.

What ticks couples off?	What makes couples tick?
Disengaging, misengaging, destructive engaging (left side of the engagement continuum)	*Engaging that meets your yearning (right side of the engagement continuum)*

Engaging on the right side is constructive and creative—it's conscious, responsible, driven by your yearnings with deeper feelings. Engaging on this side of the continuum tips your relationship ratio to the positive. You venture into the woods, going deeper into the adventure of relationship.

Awareness, consciousness, and emotional availability are the primary distinctions between the two sides. On the right side we are

ENGAGEMENT CONTINUUM

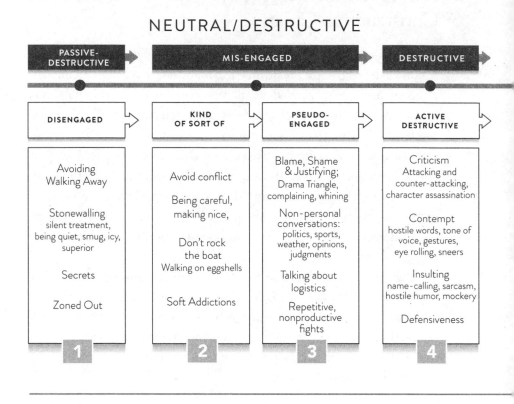

NEUTRAL/DESTRUCTIVE

PASSIVE-DESTRUCTIVE	MIS-ENGAGED		DESTRUCTIVE
DISENGAGED	**KIND OF SORT OF**	**PSEUDO-ENGAGED**	**ACTIVE DESTRUCTIVE**
Avoiding Walking Away Stonewalling silent treatment, being quiet, smug, icy, superior Secrets Zoned Out	Avoid conflict Being careful, making nice, Don't rock the boat Walking on eggshells Soft Addictions	Blame, Shame & Justifying; Drama Triangle, complaining, whining Non-personal conversations: politics, sports, weather, opinions, judgments Talking about logistics Repetitive, nonproductive fights	Criticism Attacking and counter-attacking, character assassination Contempt hostile words, tone of voice, gestures, eye rolling, sneers Insulting name-calling, sarcasm, hostile humor, mockery Defensiveness
1	2	3	4

conscious and operating with awareness and heart. The left side behaviors are largely routine or automatic. There are more integrated emotions that satisfy yearning on the right side, and we are more present and vulnerable—open to learn and grow. There is greater responsibility on this side too, which you will learn about in the "Rules of Engagement" section.

The Rules of Engagement

Fighting requires rules of engagement or it's war. We need the rules to generate the safety to engage fully. These seven rules guide you to fight

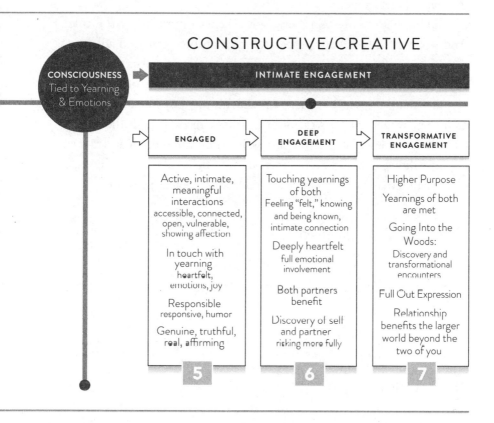

CONSTRUCTIVE/CREATIVE

CONSCIOUSNESS Tied to Yearning & Emotions

INTIMATE ENGAGEMENT

ENGAGED	DEEP ENGAGEMENT	TRANSFORMATIVE ENGAGEMENT
Active, intimate, meaningful interactions accessible, connected, open, vulnerable, showing affection	Touching yearnings of both Feeling "felt," knowing and being known, intimate connection	Higher Purpose Yearnings of both are met Going Into the Woods: Discovery and transformational encounters
In touch with yearning heartfelt, emotions, joy	Deeply heartfelt full emotional involvement	Full Out Expression
Responsible responsive, humor	Both partners benefit	Relationship benefits the larger world beyond the two of you
Genuine, truthful, real, affirming	Discovery of self and partner risking more fully	
5	**6**	**7**

productively. They facilitate creative engagement and minimize destructive interactions. We've developed and tested these during our more than thirty years of working with couples—and in our own relationship!

Empirically, we knew that couples in our program handle the bumps and bruises of relationship battles better than most, that they also experience more intimacy and satisfaction, but one survey of students confirmed this. It revealed that the divorce rate was 4 percent in our couples' training and 7 to 9 percent in our general programs. More importantly, the degree of overall satisfaction and reported love among these couples was high. They engage fully and responsibly, dancing on the engagement continuum with emphasis on the right side, following the rules of engagement.

Taking personal responsibility is the central principle of the rules. And while it's ideal if both people in a relationship agree and adhere to these rules, even if only one in the couple does this, it makes a big difference in the quality of the relationship—and often the other partner becomes more responsible, too. This isn't always easy in the heat of an argument, when you are loaded for bear and ready to pull the trigger. However, couples who use the bliss skills in our program learn to take responsibility eventually, even if it is after the fight. The rules of engagement facilitate freedom, build trust, and lead to greater intimacy.

The Rules Of Engagement

RULE #1: Accentuate the positive.

RULE #2: Minimize the negative.

RULE #3: No one gets more than 50 percent of the blame.

RULE #4: You each get 100 percent responsibility for your happiness and satisfaction.

RULE #5: Express and agree with the truth, always.

RULE #6: Fight for, not against.

RULE #7: Assume goodwill.

Rule #1: Accentuate the positive.

The dividing line from the left to the right of the engagement continuum is the orientation toward yearning. On the right-hand side, you are present and conscious, emotionally available, with responsible expression, and engaging in your deeper yearning.

Accentuate the positives in your relationship by experimenting with the categories of engaging on the right side:

Engaged delineates meaningful interactions where you are accessible, responsive, and vulnerable. You share affection, a sense of humor, and an ease of relating. You're genuine, truthful, and real with each other.

Deep Engagement touches each of your yearnings, and you both feel known and appreciated. Living with more risk, you don't hold back. You challenge each other and benefit from the straight talk.

Transformative Engagement is diving into the deep end, adventuring into the woods—discovering possibilities for yourself and your relationship. No-holds-barred, full-out expression with a higher common purpose leads to transformational encounters and breakthroughs.

Moving to the right of the engagement continuum takes some time and practice, but you'll build more intimacy and become more fulfilled. As you learn to get in touch with your yearnings and take risks in your interactions, be patient and have faith that sooner rather than later you—and your relationship—will be moving in the right direction.

Being There: Foundations for Engaging the Right Side

Engaging on the right side of the continuum meets your and your partner's yearnings, helping you build the foundation for creative engaging and lessening the limitations of the destructive. Marital researcher, Sue Johnson (2008), identified three keys to creative engagement: being *accessible*, *responsive*, and *emotionally engaged*, which means being open, attuned, and responsive to each other with emotional connection.

Are You Ready for Creative Engagement? Ask yourself the following questions to start thinking about these qualities:

Are you and your partner accessible?
Are you available for one another, and do you both feel valued?

Are you and your partner responsive?
Do you each trust that your partner will respond to you, and can you get each other's attention easily? Can you each count on the other?

Are you and your partner emotionally engaged and connected?
Do you confide in each other and show care for each other's hurts, fears, pain, anger, and joy? Do you feel close and engaged with each other?

Bidding: The Great Connection Device

You might think that we mean to get your partner to do your bidding or bid for a romantic vacation at a silent auction or on eBay for sex toys. No, bidding means you ask for attention and in turn respond to your partner's requests for attention. Our yearning to love and be loved; to be seen, heard, and known; and to matter often gets expressed as an urge that researchers call a *bid for attention*—those everyday moments when we share a thought, an observation, an "I love you," and hope or expect our partner will respond with a laugh, hug, or acknowledgment. How important is responding to bids for attention? Couples who divorce respond to only three out of ten bids compared to satisfied couples, who respond nine times out of ten (Gottman and Silver 1999).

Bids for Attention: Are You Aware?   Do you notice when your partner bids for attention? Do you ignore it, turn away from your partner, or show interest or concern in what your partner is expressing?

Imagine these scenarios and how you'd respond:

"Honey, look there's a Dairy Queen."
    a. "Did you say something?"
    b. Turn the car into the Dairy Queen parking lot and ask your spouse what topping she wants.

"Look at the hawk!"
    a. "Did you pick up the cleaning?"
    b. "Oh, wow. Show me where it is; I don't see it."

"What do you want for dinner?"
    a. "I don't care."
    b. "I really have a hankering for _____."

Your honey is snuggling up to you on the couch, but you are intently watching a football game.

    a. "Go get me a beer, would ya?"

    b. Cuddle her while you watch, or negotiate for more time, but then attend to her after the game.

Answer Key: Duh

Monitor the times you consciously accentuate the positives. Strong relationships are brimming with positive, right-side-of-the-continuum interactions. Remember, like all couples, these couples also fight. The difference is that they have more positive than negative interactions, and the destructive ones tend to decrease over time. They often tip the scales with a sense of humor and by expressing joy, affection, interest, and affirmation (Gottman 1999).

You're more likely to tip the scales to creative rather than destructive if you keep track of your interactions. Share more yearnings; express your feelings; stay present, accessible, responsive, and connected. Start experimenting with the right side of the continuum. Engage fully with truth, responsibility, genuineness, and wholehearted emotional engagement.

Keep Track as You Accentuate the Positives Evaluate yourself throughout the day by the levels of the engagement continuum from disengaged to transformative engagement. Keep a daily journal to keep track of your progress, what you are learning, how you are growing, and any changes in your relationship.

Rule #2: Minimize the negative.

Following this rule requires you recognize the range of destructive behaviors on the left side of the continuum. Be on the lookout for these categories of relationship busters: passive-destructive (disengaged), misengaging, and active-destructive.

Disengaged may sound like it is neutral, but avoiding, stonewalling, withholding, keeping secrets, or being zoned out are detrimental to you and your relationship. These passive-destructive behaviors are demonstrated relationship saboteurs.

Misengaging has two aspects. One is being *kind of sort of* there with half-hearted conversations; tiptoeing around conflict; acting nice, not real; or being checked-out with soft addictions. The other is *pseudo-engaging*: you're being active, but you're not all that conscious or aware of your yearning or your heart, and your feelings aren't engaged. Nonpersonal conversations, whether talking about politics, sports, logistics, judgments, or gossip, are part of all relationships, but if this is the predominant way you communicate, you're missing out on intimacy and you're not building your positivity ratio. Heated diatribes with blame, shame, justifying, whining, and complaining may generate a lot of energy and seem like you are relating, but these interactions don't go anywhere but to self-pity, or to building up to the next category of *active-destructive* that we'll discuss in the following sections.

Get Off Your High Horse: The Four Horsemen of the Apocalypse

One way to assess your destructive engaging behaviors can be found in John Gottman's (1999) research on the most damaging engagement styles, the Four Horsemen of the Apocalypse—communication patterns that can predict the end of a relationship: criticism, defensiveness, contempt, and withdrawal or stonewalling.

Criticism occurs when you blame, attack your partner's character or personality, or insinuate that there is something globally wrong with your partner.

Criticism paves the way for *contempt*, the second horseman and greatest predictor of divorce. Contempt shows up as sarcasm, disrespect, ridicule, eye-rolling, hostile humor, or mockery that sends messages that your partner is worthless or even despicable.

Defensiveness, the third horseman, is defending yourself from a perceived attack—you deny responsibility, make excuses, counterattack, and throw up shields in many other ways.

For years, when Bob and I would argue, I would often defend. I was sure that I was just standing up for myself. But I wouldn't acknowledge the truth of what Bob was saying and would try to push what he was saying away. He'd tell me, "You are so defensive!" to which I would ironically respond loudly: "I am not!" thereby proving that I *was* defensive.

The fourth horseman is *withdrawing* or *stonewalling*—when you shut down emotionally or physically. This can be walking away from the argument, looking away or down, not talking, not showing facial expression, keeping your defenses to yourself, and just plain being unconscious. Men often stonewall to decrease their emotional flooding, but that jacks women up, who then pursue the issue more forcefully, creating a vicious circle.

Destructive Disengaging

A particularly deceptive way couples avoid and disengage is with soft addictions (Wright 2006) or even hard ones. Checking your smartphone, surfing the Internet, indulging in television marathons, stuffing food in your mouth, chugging beers or sipping cocktails, getting lost in a video game, checking Facebook, overworking, needing alcohol or drugs for sex…are also ways that couples avoid, disengage, and withdraw. Fights of the You Love _____ More than Me type are a common manifestation of soft addiction avoidance: "You love your cell phone more than you love me!"

Rule #3: No one gets more than 50 percent of the blame.

Like it or not, we all play a part in any dynamic of our relationship; it takes two to tango! You may start an argument, but your partner may be the one who responded counterproductively, exacerbating the discord. You are always a participant in the drama or upset, even if the other person is working something through.

Perhaps you fail to communicate what you want, or actively bait your partner, or don't set limits, or nag rather than constructively act. Perhaps your partner engages in these ways. No matter who instigates the argument or makes a situation difficult, you and your partner are a part of a system, and whatever happens in the relationship, you both have a part in it. So, when you find yourself assigning blame, remind yourself that the highest percentage of blame you can assign is 50 percent.

In case you think this is too hard to do, one of our students, a grade-school teacher, has taught these rules in his classroom. He reports that his third- and fourth-grade students are applying the 50 percent rule in their arguments. For example, one student said that while fighting, she would say, "I am never going to play this game!" or "I will never be your friend." But then it would bother her all day. She now takes 50 percent of her part of the problem and says, "Yeah, I did do that." And the other student says, "I know, I did some of that too." They both take 50 percent, resolve their fight, and make friends again.

This rule sets the stage for the next rule of engagement.

Rule #4: You each get 100 percent responsibility for your happiness and satisfaction.

It is not your partner's responsibility to make you happy. It is yours alone (though of course we should support our partners). If you want something different, it is up to you to make it happen. What do you yearn for? What is it that you truly want? How do you want your relationship to be? What outcome do you desire? You want him to be more attentive or to take more responsibility for household chores—what can you do about that? You want her to stop spending so much money—what are you going to do about that? By the way, wanting to be left alone is rarely on the transformative side of the continuum.

Here's a hint: nagging, blaming, and complaining are not what it takes to change things and to make you happy. All of these are irresponsible actions. Remember, it took you years to become you and for the relationship to develop. Therefore, it is unrealistic to expect change to happen immediately. Battle strategies involve campaigns, not single conversations. Progress is made by persistence and priorities, not single actions. Continually share your yearnings and engage fully and responsibly to develop more clarity, understanding, and movement.

Rule #5: Express and agree with the truth, always.

Too often, fights rage on with a great deal of truth being said on both sides, but neither you nor your partner acknowledges it. Remarkably, many fights end when one person acknowledges the truth of what the other one is saying, because the truth is often what the person is fighting for—they yearn to be affirmed. A rule of thumb: verbally acknowledge any time your partner says something that is true—even when you are mad and don't want to give him or her the satisfaction—and if not immediately, then as soon as you recognize it. Sure, it pains you to not press your point. It may even make you look bad. Still, break the logjam and acknowledge the truth of what your partner is saying. Good words to use include the following: "You're right"; "Good point"; "I hadn't thought of it that way"; "I see your point"; or even a begrudging acknowledgment of the truth, "Screw you, do you have to be so righteous when you are right?" "Your point is right on, but I sure as hell don't like your patronizing tone"; or "Damn it, you're right, and I don't want to give you the satisfaction of acknowledging it. I'm still too mad at you."

By the same token, admit when you are wrong. Are you big enough to recognize what's right in what your partner is saying? An enormous amount of goodwill can be won by focusing on the truth and being willing to lose a fight, affirming not only the truth in what your partner is saying, but also the superiority of your partner's point or feeling. Losing is winning in this case. It's the truth that sets you free.

Rule #6: Fight *for*, not against.

Yearning is *for* things, not against them. Your partner may be doing things that irritate you or even hurt, but as challenging as it might be, the deeper yearning must be affirmed. Too often, we fight defensively about silly things or in counterproductive ways. We get sidetracked on who-said-what battles or debates over minutia. This rule of engagement requires you to have conversations where you fight *for* something other than just asserting your perspective or fighting against your partner. You recognize and own what you want and yearn for and express yourself fully and responsibly—and often, vulnerably.

This doesn't mean that the other person in your life immediately responds by giving you everything you yearn for and you never have this argument again. Instead, the point is to engage in arguments differently: with an aim. The worst arguments are filled with repeated harping, defending, nagging, avoidance, and manipulating behaviors. When you are both fighting for something, creative solutions can emerge that you never could have imagined. This is the key to win-win conflict resolution. It takes more skill and responsibility, but these genuinely responsible exchanges lead you both to be more vulnerable and open to resolution.

> **Stop and Ask Yourself**   What are you fighting for? Your answer should involve the yearning beneath the fight. Seeking the yearning is key to finding what we are fighting for. When you get to what it is that you really yearned for, get responsible and go admit to your partner what was really going on with you. You will be getting solidly reoriented for your journey into the woods.

Monitor Your Complaints   Complaining about something is not fighting for anything. Don't confuse whining and complaining with fighting *for* something, taking responsibility, and going for what you desire directly. You're probably stuck in a vicious cycle of retribution and punishment if you cannot identify what you are fighting for.

Rule #7: Assume goodwill.

Assume goodwill from your partner as opposed to ill will. That doesn't mean that sometimes you and your partner don't wish to hurt each other emotionally, whether consciously or unconsciously. Sure, if you are fully engaging, you will likely act meanly. By the same token, don't give yourself a pass if you shut down during the argument and don't "say" anything cruel. Passive-aggressive abandonment can be very punishing, so don't get too righteous if your partner made disparaging remarks and you didn't.

Assuming goodwill is a skill to learn. Make it a habit to assume goodwill and look for the positive in your partner and your relationship, rather than assuming that your partner has it out for you. So often, we scan for what our partners are doing wrong, how they don't appreciate us, or worse, how they are trying to sabotage us. And when we do that, studies show we easily miss 50 percent of the good stuff our partner is doing and perceive negativity that isn't even there (Gottman and Silver 1999)!

Studies of couples who assume ill will show that they are in a high physiological arousal state—the fight-flight-freeze mode is activated because they see their partner as an enemy or even a predator from the evil empire, rather than a friend and source of solace, support, and security. Assuming goodwill lowers this physiological arousal state, dampens the heightened sense of vigilance, and makes room for understanding and compassion (Gottman and Levenson 1988).

A Couple Becomes Engaged

Following the rules of engagement as well as the other engaging do's and don'ts takes time and persistence, so don't be discouraged if you can't get it on the first try and you find yourself still squarely on the left side of the continuum. Have faith that you, as a couple, are perfectly capable of moving from left to right, as Jake and Sadie's story illustrates.

> Jake used to come home exhausted from work, stumble into the house, barely mumble hello, go to the bathroom, then close himself in his workroom, only to come out at dinnertime. Sadie, on the other hand, ran a day care for seven children, so she could stay at home while watching her toddler; by the end of the day she was desperate for another adult to talk to and to take the toddler off her hands while she made dinner. The end of the workday transition became a time full of tension, demand, and escalating You Always/ You Never fights with Jake coming home later and later.

Sadie: You're never available. I've been waiting all day for you to get here, and you avoid us when you come home.

Jake: You never give me any credit. You are always on my case. Get off my back.

Sadie: You never listen to me! You don't give a damn about what's going on with me! I've been home with two-year-olds, speaking three-word sentences. My brain is drying up. You have an office. You've been with grown-ups all day.

Jake: Why should I come home...to listen to all this shit with you ragging on me every night? You're such a bitch.

> Jake and Sadie were committed to making the relationship work, and they began moving themselves to the right of the engagement continuum during their You Always/You Never fights.
> Right off the bat, they made the effort to identify what they truly *yearned* for. Sadie realized that she really yearned to matter as

a woman, not just a mother who meets the many demands of her toddler, and to be connected to herself, to Jake, and to the larger world. Jake, after a good deal of probing, grasped that he yearned to feel more centered, peaceful, and secure—more together—which called for him to shake off the tensions of the day and to share more with Sadie.

Then they began to *engage*—acting on their yearnings and becoming more responsible. They began to use the rules of engagement, taking responsibility and not dumping all the blame on each other. They began fighting *for* yearning fulfillment, for changes that worked for both of them. They began to problem solve and acknowledge the truth of what the other was saying, rather than batting each other's responses away.

Jake took responsibility for coming home in good shape. He realized that he was arriving home in a foul mood, but without telling Sadie what was going on at work and why he was so stressed. He came home upset and angry, treating Sadie worse than the way the boss he loathed treated him. Sadie saw new ways to meet her needs for adult contact; she made an effort to feel part of a world bigger than herself and the toddlers in her care.

When they both got out of their drama triangle and got to their yearning, they found innovative solutions. They worked together and experimented with different options to change the charged situation. For instance, Sadie hired a neighborhood teenager to sit with their toddler so she could have time to herself—whether it was to have a cup of tea, go to the gym, call a friend, sit outside, or read a book—before she started dinner.

Jake exercised after work to blow off steam rather than steaming when he came home. He arrived at the house in a better mood, looking forward to seeing his wife and his son, rather than resenting one more demand on him. They became more caring and appreciative, even when they had one of their You Always/You Never fights. After dinner and playing with Jake, they alternated who read bedtime stories, did the nighttime rituals, and tucked the toddler into bed. They became more insistent on his regular bedtime because they started to cherish their couple time together, catching up on their days, sharing the frustrations and their successes, enjoying each other's company—or having a fight without the nastiness of their former You Always/You Never fights thrown in. Now, they were able to argue, air their differences, and get realigned. Unbeknownst to them, they were changing their neurochemistry.

Better Living and Loving Through Chemistry

Neuroscience research shows that we can create an amazing chemistry within and between us by living on the right side of the continuum and using the rules of engagement. When we are on the left side of the continuum experiencing criticism or rejection, or feeling minimized, we produce higher levels of feel-bad stress hormones. It's almost like being under the influence of Harry Potter's Dementors, who drain happiness and positive emotions. The hormones shut down the thinking center of your brain, activate conflict aversion, and trigger protection behaviors. It decreases your ability to connect, have empathy, and think creatively. You become more sensitive and more reactive, see more negativity and judgment from your partner than actually exists, and miss at least half of the positives in your relationship (Glaser and Glaser 2014).

But when you are on the right side of the continuum, the neuro-chemical wash creates relationship magic. Positive comments and conversations trigger the production of oxytocin, which increases your trust and elevates your ability to communicate by activating networks in your prefrontal cortex. Your ability to connect, feel empathy, and think creatively is heightened (Glaser and Glaser 2014). Receptors throughout your body flood with oxytocin, promoting attachment and connection; producing calm, close, tranquil, and loving feelings; lessening your anxiety and stress; and improving your relationship skills (Moberg 2003). But oxytocin's effects don't last as long as cortisol in our metabolism, which may explain why we need to create more frequent "hits" (five positives to every negative) on the right side of the continuum.

The chemistry of engaging the right way facilitates good battles. Instead of being defensive when our partner points out a shortcoming, we are open and objective. Instead of focusing solely on our problems, we are able to be supportive of the issues our spouse is dealing with. Instead of being sadistic when pointing out faults, we are able to offer constructive and even loving criticism.

On the right side of the continuum, when you show concern for your partner or are truthful about what's on your mind or exhibit other positive engaging behaviors, you boost your oxytocin and increase your trust, well-being, and loving attitude. When you live more on the right side of the continuum, using the rules of engagement, you are living in love.

Learning how to engage properly allows our brains to supply us with oxytocin rather than cortisol. We don't just feel better, we—and our relationships—*are* better, which encourages us to keep engaging fully, consciously, and deeply. This leads us to learn and share on a journey of discovery and disclosure, *revealing*, even as we are engaged in an argument with the one we love—the next skill.

CHAPTER 6

Reveal

Uncover the Matrix of Your Unconscious Beliefs and Unfinished Business

Most couples think their fights are about the topic of the fight: "If you'd just put the dishes away…stop spending so much money… get off your cell phone…just change." When we focus on the surface, we miss what is really going on in our fights and in our relationship. If you don't dive deep beneath what's evident, especially when you're engaged in conflict, you won't discover the real causes operating beneath your awareness, and you'll miss the rich life hidden in the depths. It's like looking at the surface of the ocean compared to author Dave Barry's (1989) reflection on diving beneath the water:

> [W]hen you finally see what goes on underwater, you realize that you've been missing the whole point of the ocean. Staying on the surface all the time is like going to the circus and staring at the outside of the tent.

For instance, John is generally thoughtful when he's running late, but on the ten times or so a year that he forgets to call and let her know, Mary goes to war, saying he's Mr. Big Shot and thinks he's too good to call. What's really going on, however, is that unbeknownst to Mary, unconscious material from her past is surfacing in this fight. Growing up, Mary felt profoundly hurt by her father's absence. Worse yet he always found time to be with her older brother, but claimed work kept him too busy to spend time with her. John's infrequent inconsideration was about way more than notifying her or coming home on time.

Mary's unconscious belief that she did not matter was emerging in the fight. We refer to the complex of beliefs and other unconscious elements that govern our feelings and thoughts as our *matrix*. *Revealing*, the third bliss skill, is about looking beneath the fight to recognize the limiting beliefs and other elements that make up your matrix. To reveal means that you discover your limiting beliefs, programming, unconscious motivations, and deeper truths—and that you share or reveal these, becoming more genuine, authentic, and transparent.

You discover what makes you and your partner tick and what ticks you both off and why. You get to the heart of the fight and discover why it bugs you so much when he leaves clothes on the floor, or what is really going on beneath his penchant for tidiness, or your anger at your partner's money habits. As you begin to understand yourself and your partner better, you realize what drew you to each other, your unconscious hopes and expectations, and how these affect your interactions— and trigger fights. Rather than simply wanting your partner to change so you aren't so upset, you learn to use your upsets in the relationships to learn more about yourself and each other.

Your relationship becomes a continual source of exciting discovery as you go beneath the surface to the heart of the fight.

What ticks couples off?	What makes couples tick?
Defending false fronts	Revealing more of themselves
Unconscious triggers from the past or projecting past relationships onto each other	Discovering—and sharing—what is going on deep inside them
Tail-chasing, circular fights that don't get below the surface	Getting to what is really going on beneath a fight

Blame It on the Matrix: How It Is—Is How It *Was*

This skill leads you to recognize and understand the unconscious elements of fights. Your unconscious mind is a *million* times more powerful than your conscious mind (Norretranders 1998). Your conscious mind's prefrontal cortex alone processes forty nerve impulses per second, while 90 percent of your unconscious brain processes 40 *million* nerve impulses per second (Lipton 2013).

In the beginning of our relationships, we often experience the *honeymoon effect* (Lipton 2013)—we're more likely to be in the present moment, paying conscious attention to our lover, which brings us much more excitement and satisfaction. But as day-to-day reality sets in, the unconscious mind takes over, directed by early, often subconscious programming, and unfinished business from the past surfaces—often with strong emotion that frequently results in fights.

> Michael grew up with an unreasonable father; as a child he felt intimidated and unable to stand up to him. In the present, he is married to Sally, who is a strong woman and can be firm with Michael. When she behaves in a strong-willed way and won't back down, Michael explodes. He plays the Blame Game and accuses her of being self-centered and "making him upset."
>
> Though Michael seems to be battling about an issue that involves the current state of their marriage, he actually has been triggered by the firm stance that Sally has taken—it reminds him of his father and how he could never stand up to him. So, he explodes at her today with a force built up from his past. Neither Michael nor Sally is consciously aware of what is really going on.

The Forming of the Matrix

The effect of our past on our present relationships, though, is more complex than this example suggests. As infants, our brains are "wired" through our interactions with our parents, creating the neuropathways of our matrix that underlay a complex of unconscious beliefs, feelings, and behavior patterns—our sense of self, beliefs about ourselves, what the world expects from us, and what we can expect from the world. During the first seven years of life, you were downloading the program that will continue to run your life if you do not consciously change your complex of unconscious governing beliefs. In our example above, when Sally is firm, Michael explodes, expecting Sally to be unreasonable and unyielding like his father was. He is really fighting an unconscious memory of his father embedded in his matrix, not Sally.

The matrix, with its unconscious beliefs, colors our thoughts, feelings, perceptions, and actions—and our relationship choices. It controls how we engage with others, how comfortable or uncomfortable we are with intimacy, and how triggered we get when our loved one isn't available. It determines our emotional tenor and what sparks our fights—all from our early experiences (Wright and Wright 2013).

While there's nothing you can do about your past, you can do a lot about your present. No one had an absolutely perfect childhood. It is your job as an adult in relationships to learn where your gaps are, and to take responsibility to fill them in and continue where your childhood development left off.

Implicit Memory—in the Present from the Past

This early matrix encoded in our neural circuitry works almost entirely within our implicit memory, which means it is outside of our conscious awareness. Implicit memories are stored sensations and feelings, which aren't attached to an explicit event or memory in time. Early memories are formed before we have language, logical thought, or explicit recall (Siegel 2012a). Chances are you don't remember exact incidents when your parent picked you up in your crib and reassured you as you cried or how often your diapers were changed, what you wore, how your mother smelled, the color of your bedroom, or what lullaby your father sang to you. It is only within the middle of our second year that we start to develop explicit memory where we remember specific incidents and details.

Why does all this matter? Because while implicit memories from the past are stored outside of our awareness, they arise in the present moment, and are masked by what we think we are experiencing in the current moment. Our matrix shapes our present experiences from the implicit foundation. When we are angry, panicking, or feeling deeply hurt, our present feelings often stem from our implicit memories, and we assume the present situation is causing our reaction.

When strong implicit memories are triggered, unbeknownst to us, childhood pain and fear come raging to the surface. This may happen when you sense your partner isn't there for you, for instance, and you don't have a clue that you just activated a pain pocket from your matrix through an implicit memory. You think your charged emotional reaction is all due to your partner's insensitivity, and while that is a trigger, the bulk of the charge is coming from the past.

I get really hurt and angry when I can't get Bob's attention—it seems to me he is purposefully ignoring me, and on a scale of one (no biggie, doesn't bother me) to ten (being super plugged in and upset), I'm reacting with an eight. Now that I know to practice this skill and look underneath the anger to what's triggering me—I realize that about six of those eight points are from my past and two are from the immediate interaction with Bob. The part of me that is so sad, hurt, angry, and feeling powerless is the little "ghost child" of my past, the "me" who felt invisible a lot of the time and powerless to do anything about it.

Revealing requires learning to recognize reactions that are out of proportion to present events. When we bring this to conscious awareness, we can understand what is really going on with us, why fights often feel so stupid on the surface, and what unfinished business needs to be tended to.

Rate Your Charge   Take something that really bothers you in your relationship, that you really dislike or even hate about your partner.

Rate how similar your charge and the situation are to past events from your family of origin or childhood from 1 to 10:

1 = I have never experienced anything remotely like this before (almost certainly denial).

10 = This feels really familiar, so I know this full charge isn't all from my partner. My past is influencing my reaction. I am putting my mother's (father's) face on my partner right now, and she or he has little or nothing to do with how reactive I am being.

Recognizing Core Beliefs About Yourself and the World

You may find it upsetting that the raging set-to you just had with your spouse is a product of something that happened thirty years ago. But there's a difference between the limiting beliefs that govern our behaviors and what is possible. Your perceived limits are often not inherently true but stem from faulty wiring that you can learn to fix. Later in the book we'll explain how you can fix it, but first you need to make the connection between feelings, attitudes, and unconscious beliefs.

Once you understand how you were wired as a kid, it's easy to see how we all form limiting beliefs about ourselves and the world. It's not just troubled or dysfunctional families or bad parenting. It's the nature of our development. Early on, we don't even have language or logic to make sense of our experience. For instance, when we are babies and our mom has a lot on her mind, is under a lot of pressure, and is irritated when she feeds us or tends to our needs, we have a mix of feelings and sensations associated with that experience that are encoded as beliefs about ourselves and our world. We don't have the logic or reason to say, "Oh, Mom's just tired; really, she loves me," or "Dad's irritable about the pressures in his job; it's not me." We are absorbing these experiences with no filter.

Not only do you have limiting familial programming, but our culture provides limiting programming too. In order to tap your full potential for intimacy and fulfillment in relationships, you need to break the spell of both family and societal beliefs regarding relationships, emotions, possibilities, and acceptable behavior. You might not recognize many of these beliefs since you attribute your thoughts, feelings, and actions to everyday occurrences, missing the implicit memories that are being stirred up. Regardless, here is a list of feelings, thoughts, and attitudes and some of the corresponding unconscious limiting beliefs that underlay them.

LIMITING BELIEFS

I feel... I think... I act...	My unconscious, mistaken core beliefs may be...
• Insecure • Inferior • Superior (to overcompensate for feelings of inferiority) • No matter what I do, it's not enough • Relationships are fragile • I can't handle it • Scared to take risks • Trying to prove myself, prove that I am okay	• I'm not enough. • I'm not good enough. • I'm not okay.
• Holding back • Toning down my expressions • My partner can't handle me if I am really myself	• I'm too much.
• Think you have to be certain ways in order to be loved—perfect, pretty, wealthy, successful, nice, smart...	• I have to earn love. • I'm not loveable (for who I am).

I feel... I think... I act...	My unconscious, mistaken core beliefs may be...
· Can't depend on others · Don't ask for help · Asking for help is weak · I have to do things myself	· I'm alone and on my own.
· Can't ask for what I want · Often settle for less than I deserve · Sacrifice my needs for others · Don't speak up	· I'm not worthy. · I don't matter.
· I have to be happy all the time · Anger is bad and to be hidden or suppressed · Don't be sad	· My feelings are bad or wrong.
· Needy	· I'm a burden.
· I don't have enough energy, time, or money · There's not enough love to go around	· I live in a scarce world. There aren't enough resources.
· I have to give more than I get · Can't count on others	· The world is not here to support me. · The world doesn't want what is best for me.
· Others have ill will toward me · Constantly scanning for threats · Defensive · Constantly strategize worst-case scenarios	· The world is out to get me. · The world is a hostile place.
· Scared to take risks	· The world is dangerous.

Identify the Limiting Beliefs in Your Fights Review the chart. What characteristics, thoughts, feelings, and behaviors do you have, and what mistaken beliefs do they indicate? See which apply to you and surface in your fights.

Picking a Perfect Prick

No, we're not putting down your choice of a mate. We want you to recognize the perfection of your partner, especially in the way he pricks your unfinished business. Harville Hendrix (2007) asserts that our unconscious mind is working overtime to choose a complement to ourselves, someone to activate our matrix. Your matrix includes unconscious forces that propel you to love and to war with your partner, including your attachment schemas, limiting beliefs, and implicit memories.

You're predisposed to choose someone who is most likely to trigger your mistaken beliefs about yourself and the world, poke at old emotional wounds, or even rub metaphorical salt in them. They will bring to the surface any aspects of yourself that you haven't integrated or haven't discovered.

No, this isn't some bad cosmic joke—instead of being destined to fall in love with a fairy-tale prince or princess, you're destined to spend your life with a great sparring partner. If you want a full, engaged life, then you need that partner. The unconscious purpose of relationships is to complete or continue our development and provoke us to learn, grow, and even transform ourselves. Remember, attraction isn't just about chemistry. You wouldn't have been attracted to someone or "fallen in love" unless she or he fit your unconscious template of what love "feels" like—the good and the bad.

We all have a conscious stated reason for getting into relationships: we fell in love; we want to share our life with a special someone; we can't imagine living without him or her. But there is also an unconscious purpose of relationships: to complete our unfinished developmental business and become the person we can become. Fights often occur because unfinished business is rising to the surface. This serves a purpose: it helps you become conscious of what needs to be faced, understood, and shared for you to learn, grow, and complete yourself.

Transference and Projection: Who's That in My Bed?

In the beginning of relationships, we unconsciously and consciously project positive, wished-for attributes onto our partner: *He'll love me for who I am. She'll accept and respect me. He'll provide the security I never had. She'll make me feel alive and special. He has the family I always needed.* We engage in positive projection because we expect someone to provide our solidity, self-acceptance, aliveness, or even our success.

But then something breaks that positive projection—we see that our partner isn't the ideal person we had thought, conflict emerges, our unconscious material begins to surface, implicit memories from our matrix emerge, and we begin to project negative traits onto our partner. This wonderful, caring person metamorphoses into an uncaring, cavalier, insensitive, rejecting, or cruel person—whatever traits are associated with our implicit memories of important people from our past.

This often erupts in You've Changed fights. While people do change, your own change in projection is what's powerfully unsettling. Every relationship we have involves projection and transference, terms from Freudian and developmental psychology that describe our unconscious redirection of feelings from a childhood relationship to one that affects our relationships in the present. One of our students articulated the relationship between the anger that catalyzed her fights and projection:

> There was a time when my whole worldview and perspective changed when I learned about projections. I began to see that there was no one out there but me. My husband and every person that I was really mad at, hated, blamed, and even admired was just an aspect of myself that I was projecting. After this, I literally

began to treat him and others differently and began to get to know myself for the first time (Wright 2008).

Learning to reclaim projections is key to intimacy and unlocking fights. You can't be intimate with someone you don't know or can't see, which is what happens when you coat your experience of them with your past. Intimacy also requires knowing yourself and that means recognizing how you create your reality based on forces from the past.

When I realized how much I had made Bob pay for wrongs he didn't commit, I was truly remorseful. I realized that I was punishing him because of people in my past that I transferred onto him. I hadn't been seeing Bob for who he was. I had been interpreting his behaviors from my past schema, often coating him with a negative wash, ascribing negative motivations to him that weren't his, "hearing" a tone of voice that wasn't there. Once I started reclaiming my projections and understanding what was really getting triggered for me, I could take it back to the source, rather than project onto Bob. Now I am more conscious of my projections; I notice when my charges and reactions are beyond what the situation calls for; I am more able to see what is going on. More importantly, I am clearer and more conscious, and can more accurately see Bob for who he is, and appreciate and love him even more fully.

Reclaim Your Projection: Find Your Triggers from the Past Use the following questions to discover your projection or transference from your past when you have a strong charge or reaction in the present.

- *What's this to me?*
- *What about this bothers me so much?*
- *What feels familiar about this?*
- *When did I feel this way before?*
- *Who does this remind me of?*
- *What mistaken belief is triggered?*

Now, go share the results of this exercise with your partner.

Law of Complementarity and Unconscious Contracts

The law of complementarity—choosing partners who can provide what we don't provide for ourselves—is driven by unconscious projection, as the following example demonstrates. Without being consciously aware, we "contract" with that person to play a certain complementary role in our lives.

> When Joe first met Faye, he was fascinated by her expressive, imaginative style of talking. She was so creative and alive and very different from his law school friends and the people who were part of his stuffy upbringing. Faye loved and was really attracted to Joe's solidity and rationality; she felt safe and secure when she was with him.
>
> Growing up as the third born of five in a rather dour and serious family, Faye was told that she was flighty, too sensitive, emotional, and dramatic. Joe, a first-born of two, grew up in a family of battling parents and was the apple of his mother's eye and the pride of the family.
>
> Faye represented an emotional complement to Joe's rationality, and Joe represented a rational complement to Faye's emotionality. This relationship is a typical example of the law of complementarity. They engaged in an initial unconscious *contract* from their first meeting: Faye provides the aliveness for Joe, and Joe provides the stability for Faye. But over time, Joe found Faye's ways irritating and Faye felt like Joe's stolid nature was not only boring but limiting their lives. Seemingly overnight, they started detesting each other. Each hated what they formerly loved about the other—erupting in I Can't Stand the Way You _____ fights.
>
> Cringing at her flights of fancy, rolling his eyes at her exuberance, and judging her as crazy, Joe exasperatedly would yell, "Stop it. Shut up! I can't stand the way you go on and on about nothing!"

Faye would reply: "Oh, yeah, I can't stand that you never show any enthusiasm about anything. You are such a lump! It's like living with Mr. Spock. You wouldn't know a feeling if it bit you in the ass."

What initially brought Joe and Faye together will eventually divide them, unless they consciously learn to shift the initial contract and overcome the power of the law of complementarity by learning and growing into what they wanted from each other.

Revealing is about discovering this law of complementarity and understanding the unfinished business that each person brings to the relationship. Self-acceptance was a key lesson for Faye. What Faye thought she was finding in Joe was acceptance of her emotional sensitivity and expressive, creative ways. However, eventually Joe would reject her for these traits and find her irritating; the revealing process, in response, led Faye to develop more self-acceptance. Joe, on the other hand, needed to learn to be more spontaneous, realizing that his brother's wildness when they were growing up was a lot more fun than his own lifestyle and that Faye represented an aliveness that he needs to tap within himself for his continued growth and development.

Fortunately, Joe and Faye used the bliss skills to reveal, discovering how the law of complementarity played out in their unspoken contract, revealing unfinished business for each. Rather than continuing to rely on the other to provide what they lacked, they began to fulfill their own needs.

Joe started to see his overintellectualizing and his control issues and admitted how tightly wound he was, trying to make everything perfect and be the good boy in his family, and how deadening and exhausting that had become. He revealed that he actually envied Faye's freedom and resented that she knew how to have more fun than he did. He yearned to feel that freedom to be whatever felt good and not just "do" the right thing.

Faye admitted that she was unnecessarily flighty some times, just to try to get a rise out of Joe. She shared her hurt and anger from her childhood, admitting that she felt like she needed to perform to get any attention, even the critical kind. She continually tried to lighten up her overserious family, and then she was reviled for being flighty. Her family would get more uptight and distant in response to her flightiness, which would only escalate her flights of fantasy as she felt increasingly abandoned and insecure, resenting that they controlled her instead of encouraging her—exactly what Joe would try to do.

Realizing and sharing these insights with one another brought them much closer. They started to understand themselves and each other—learning new ways of thinking and growing in empathy and an even stronger desire to change their own patterns. They were revealing.

> **Discover Your Unspoken Contracts** Find as many unconscious contracts as you can in your present and past relationships. Who played what roles? Where have you been disillusioned? What did you hope your partner would provide for you? What was your unspoken contract when you got together? For example: Was he supposed to be the solid one and you the lively one? Or was she to be the competent one and you the playful one?
>
> It may help you to reflect on other couples you know. Their patterns and unspoken or even spoken agreements may be easier to see than your own.

Screaming Schemas

Are you comfortable with closeness, or does intimacy make you squirm?

Your answer gives you a clue to your attachment schema, the unconscious implicit programming that colors your relationships (Bowlby 1969). You'll be better equipped to resolve relationship conflict productively if you understand your attachment pattern and your partner's. Knowing your and your partner's attachment styles can help you understand and empathize more when you realize your partner is not consciously intending to hurt or ignore you. This understanding can help you relax when bugged. You reflect, *He's insecure about my love for him. It's not that I don't love him enough.* Your partner is operating on an unconscious attachment pattern (one that you were originally attracted to, by the way). Attachment schemas indicate unfinished developmental business to be addressed for personal transformation and relationship success.

Under all of the attachment styles lie the yearnings for connection and security, but we deal with them differently depending on our early experiences and resulting schemas.

Do You Tend to Avoid Closeness?

If you tend to avoid getting too close, your early years of growing up didn't provide optimal connection and attachment. You may have been ignored, punished, or disapproved of when you expressed your needs or were vulnerable. You might also have had a smothering, enmeshed relationship. Either way, going toward connection was painful and unsuccessful, so today you sidestep the pain by avoiding connection. You shun closeness because it's too uncomfortable to get close, or too painful.

If you dismiss closeness because you deem it as needy or unnecessary, or you're self-sufficient, it is highly unlikely you would be reading this book, because you wouldn't be concerned about your relationship and you'd figure it is the other person's problem. You tend to think you are worthy of love but don't believe that others are willing or capable.

Whether you avoid closeness out of fear or dismissal, you *deactivate* your attachment system to avoid the pain.

This can show up in subtle ways—wanting "space," walking a stride ahead of a partner on the sidewalk, not wanting to be "controlled," blowing hot and cold, preferring solo activities, having difficulty saying "I love you" or sharing emotions and vulnerability, fantasizing about someone else during sex to keep distant (Levine and Heller 2010). It can also be projected with you thinking the distance is due to your partner.

Do You Desire Closeness but Don't Trust Others Will Be There, or Do You Fear You'll Be Rejected?

You yearn for connection, but in your childhood, when these patterns were established, you couldn't count on your caregiver being there consistently and responding to you and your needs appropriately. In adulthood, you worry whether your partner will be available, attentive, or responsive. You may also become agitated, hurt, or angry when your partner withdraws.

You don't feel secure about being loved and loveable. You *hyperactivate* your attachment system and often make somewhat desperate attempts to get attention and affection from your partner, becoming angry and resentful when he or she is unresponsive (Shaver and Mikulincer 2002). This can manifest in many ways: whining, begging, excessive texting, "gamey" or seductive behavior; in your partner, it can manifest as playing games, expecting you to mind read or guess what is going on, fighting, or even punishing, critical behavior.

Warring Attachment Patterns

These two patterns—avoiding connection and making frantic attempts to get reassurance and affection from your partner—can result in seemingly irreconcilable fights with vicious circles of one partner avoiding, the other scrambling for connection, which triggers more avoiding and more scrambling. You can rise above the conflict by digging underneath it; you can see what resides behind clinging and avoiding behaviors and use this information to grow.

What Are Both of Your Attachment Schemas? What attachment schema seems most like yours? Your partner's? Do you avoid or cling, or are you somewhere in between? Discuss the implications of these in your relationship and in your fights with your partner.

Luckily, as we learn the bliss skills, we can create increasingly secure attachments and develop what researchers call "earned secure attachment" regardless of the type of attachment we experienced as children (Siegel 2012a). We become comfortable with closeness and learn to trust that our partner will be there for us.

Attachment Breaches: Flipping Our Lids!

No matter what your attachment style, the threat of lost attachment, called breaches—rifts in our relationship—often trigger highly emotional fights. For Bob, the breach happens when Judith withdraws. For Judith, it's when Bob doesn't pay attention to her. In each case, attachment breaches send us into upsets we refer to as amygdala hijacks. Your amygdala "hijacks" your thinking mind (Goleman 2006) and triggers default behaviors—the behaviors that your early attachment experiences programmed in your matrix. You have "flipped your lid," overridden your prefrontal cortex and lost its clear reasoning (Siegel 2010, 22). You avoid, scramble for attention, freeze, flee, or freak out in other ways.

While its function is important, the hair-trigger amygdala can be sloppy and distort things in this quick reaction. We lose rational perspective (Siegel 2010). The amygdala within the limbic system responds even before our frontal lobe or neocortex perceives a threat. The amygdala sends a rush of adrenaline and cortisol that signals the body to fight, flee, or freeze. This release of chemicals into the brain reduces our working memory and stops complex thought. Our limbic system doesn't want us to take the time to think—it just wants us to fight, flee, or freeze! This survival mechanism lets us react to things before the rational brain has time to mull things over (Siegel 2010). Our breaches often trigger one another in this way. When Bob ignores Judith, she feels hurt and withdraws, and her withdrawal can send Bob into a rage.

Name It to Tame It In these instances, take a step back and say to yourself, *Whoa, what's going on with me? Why am I so triggered (angry, enraged, freaked out, frozen, numb, shut down, or charged up)? Ah, that's it; I'm in an amygdala hijack.* If you can have this type of self-awareness and learn how to act differently in these situations, you can reveal and eventually liberate yourself from this reactive loop. You will give yourself the option of choosing a new and better behavior. Don't doubt you can do this; students as early as third grade are identifying hijacks to avert conflict.

Unfinished Business Concealed Beneath Your False Self

Revealing provides a powerful foundation for self-discovery. When you unpack your fights, you will recognize historic patterns and lessons to learn that stem from your earliest years. You can then work on your unconscious, unfinished business.

We all have unfinished business—the limiting beliefs of our matrix, our attachment schemas, implicit memory, projections, and transferences—that often trigger our fights or avoidances. Our fights indicate a need to acknowledge, understand, accept, and complete unfinished business. This invariably means learning lessons we've avoided or not even recognized.

Our unfinished business is often hidden underneath the shield of what Freud called our ego ideal and others call our false self (Winnicott 1965), the self we show the world and want the world to validate. We are taught that only certain parts of ourselves are okay, so those become the only parts we show.

We disown many of the other parts, thinking these parts are bad or aren't loveable, and we hide them from others or even ourselves. We conceal unacceptable aspects of ourselves: our criticisms, emotions, pain, or even joy. So the only parts of us that we present to others are the acceptable parts in our false self. And people close to us, like our partner, are likely to see and stir up the parts that don't fit our ego ideal.

We begin to finish our unfinished business as we acknowledge and reclaim these disowned parts of ourselves. These are often revealed in You're Just Like Your Mother/Father fights (pick your favorite—father, sister, grandfather, brother). As these parts of ourselves are identified, we generally want to defend and say, "I am not." But we are, and we have denied the ways we are like our family members though our partner sees them very clearly. We need to own and integrate all aspects of ourselves, especially those in the shadow of our false self, in order to be whole, to develop, to become who we can become, and to have robust relationships.

A criticism of Bob from his mother was, "You're just like your father"—or "uncle," or "grandfather." It took him years to reclaim and integrate the aspects of each he had tried to suppress because they seemed unacceptable.

Denying any part of ourselves, even the most unattractive or undesirable, keeps us from experiencing our greatest intimacy. Many of us live in fear of being unmasked as insufficient, "He says he loves me, but if he really knew this about me, he'd never love and want me." And to the extent that we try to hide these parts of ourselves, we fight to avoid discovery.

When your partner accuses you of being picky, unloving, mean, or whatever it is that you have denied about yourself, fights can escalate pretty quickly as you try to protect your false self. The result: surface-level disputes or avoidances. Our fights become irresponsible or messy attempts to protect our false self, generally by blaming our partner.

Think about something your partner has accused you of that really made you mad or hurt your feelings. Chances are that your strong reaction came from it spotlighting something that you think is terrible about yourself. This is a clue to your false self.

When Bob would tell me I was being mean, I would become very defensive and bat it away with a series of justifications and often counterattacks. To me, being mean was horrible. "I'm a nice person, how could I be mean?" Being mean meant that I wasn't lovable or even okay. I wanted Bob, and everyone else, to see me as "nice," kind, thoughtful, empathic, caring, and sensitive. Thanks to revealing, I recognized that I didn't need to be so nice all the time; I could let myself get openly and honestly pissed off, be mean, and cop to it, rather than denying, defending, "Oh, I didn't mean it," or some other BS excuse.

I keep taking the next step in letting more of myself show—from snippy comments to full-blooded anger. Ironically, I've become more trustworthy because what you see is what you get. I'm not simmering on the inside and acting nice on the outside; I'm more congruent—and more real. And I also feel more seen and am even more adored. Bob likes "bad Judith" (no, not what you're thinking) when I let my judgments out, express my strong opinions, and am straight talking—the very things I used to criticize Bob for! Now when he calls me a bitch, I say, "Thank you, I've worked hard on that."

Identify: What Are You Hiding and Protecting? To stop protecting your false self, learn to identify the parts of yourself that you hide. Start by rank-ordering the five primary emotions below in order of most acceptable to least acceptable:

Joy, Sadness, Anger, Hurt, Fear

The least acceptable is a good place to start looking for what your false self is shielding, also known as your denied or shadow self.

Now think about other traits you hide or try to minimize like the following.

Critical, Gossipy, Sensitive, Strong, Weak, Emotional, Afraid, Hurtful

You're hiding, minimizing, or denying these traits because you think they are not okay and you're not okay when you are these ways. Intimacy requires that we engage in the process of reclaiming as much of our denied selves as we can. Consider asking friends for feedback, too.

Going All the Way: Get Naked— Reveal Yourself for Better Intercourse

Get naked! Sounds like a good prescription for better intimacy—and it works both in bed and out. Remember, revealing means uncovering your unfinished business and that includes baring your soul, getting emotionally naked, and revealing more of yourself. As your fights tease up feelings, childhood triggers, and unfinished business beneath the surface, you share them.

Let your guard down, be vulnerable, share yourself—yup, all of you. Share the messy, upsetting, embarrassing parts; the tender feelings, the unrecognized anger, the unacknowledged fear; the long-forgotten childhood incidents and memories, the secrets you want to keep, the parts of yourself you don't want anyone to see. If you are being an irresponsible shit in a fight, admit it. If your feelings are hurt, say ouch. If you are punishing your partner with the silent treatment, fess up. If you're pissed, say so. If you're afraid, cop to it. If you're feeling warm and tender, say it—and show it. If you don't know what's going on, own up to that.

Getting to—and sharing—what is going on underneath the surface of your fights can be one of the most powerful features of intimacy in your relationship. Sharing these vulnerable discoveries creates some of the most powerful intimate encounters and some of the best intercourse of all kinds!

Now you see your fights not as a problem, but as a powerful doorway to self-knowledge, growth, deep understanding, and intimacy as you unearth the unconscious layers that trigger them. As you dig deeper, you and your partner will unlock your fights, understand yourself and each other better, become more empathic, and get even closer as you battle to bliss.

You're going all the way, diving deeply into the unknown, trusting that you will uncover the limiting beliefs of your matrix and your unfinished business. You share the journey to discover the richness of your denied and hidden selves. Now you are ready to pay the price and reap the benefits—changing your thinking, feeling, and doing. You are ready to *liberate*—to become your full, genuine self—freeing yourself from limiting beliefs, experiencing new ways of living as you complete your unfinished business and forge a new you and a new relationship.

CHAPTER 7

Liberate

Break Free from Limiting Beliefs and Behaviors

When you *liberate*, the fourth bliss skill, you think the unthinkable, say the unsayable, and do what may have seemed impossible before. You *break free* from the matrix of limiting beliefs you discovered in revealing. You *free yourself to be your best self* and to create new relationships with yourself and others. Liberating is not for the faint of heart; it requires awareness, risk, and audacity—but what worthy challenge doesn't?

Liberating is key to a new paradigm of relationship—a transformational paradigm of adventure where we grow and transform into new ways of being with our partners. Liberating challenges two areas of limiting beliefs that you uncover as you engage and reveal: beliefs about yourself and beliefs about relationships, including fighting and intimacy. In this model, the purpose of a relationship is not to find the right partner but to be the right partner, where you both are working toward something greater and becoming all you can be.

It's time to break out of your old habits of relating and start fighting for what you, and your relationship, could be. Risk. Experiment. Fight for what really matters—not just to feel better, but to *be* better. Break free from your matrix and limiting beliefs. Experiment and act on more empowering beliefs. With liberating, you're not just fighting to get your spouse to put the cap on the toothpaste or for your partner to agree to more sex; you're fighting to assert your own entitlement, to matter, to show respect and care for each other. You are fighting for your potential and to discover what is possible in your relationship.

Free to Love

Breaking free to be yourself requires just that, freedom to be. Virginia Satir (1976), the famed couples and family therapist of the human potential movement, espoused five freedoms that can guide you in liberating—what we hope you'll experience in your fights and in your relationship as you liberate:

- the freedom to *see and hear what is here* instead of what should be, was, or will be

- the freedom to *say what you feel and think*, instead of what you should

- the freedom to *feel what you feel*, instead of what you ought

- the freedom to *ask for what you want*, instead of always waiting for permission

- the freedom *to take risks on your own behalf*, instead of choosing to be only "secure" and not rocking the boat

As you learn to live these freedoms, you will automatically be yearning, engaging, and revealing new discoveries that indicate a new direction for your liberating.

Breaking Free One Doable Task at a Time

Even though exercising these freedoms requires venturing into the unknown, liberating isn't about big huge leaps. You start with small, focused steps. You will learn the strategy to repeat these for lasting change, *rematrixing*, in the next chapter. For now, focus on engaging to challenge limiting beliefs.

Liberating happens in small steps in the behaviors most available to you—thinking the next riskier thought, saying a little more truth, going one step further into a conflict, making the next move to break your old relating habits. Your intent activates your ability to grow new neural circuitry of beliefs, thoughts, and behaviors, guided by your revealing insights. You'll stretch just a bit, right at the edge of your comfort zone but not totally beyond it, by doing something new and different. This "wakes up" your brain and signals it to pay attention (Rock and Schwartz 2006).

Stretching into that next doable step can make a huge difference, as Dave and Hildy discovered. Hildy was upset and loaded for bear, intent on duking it out with Dave. They started a Dueling Over Dollars fight and shifted it midstream with a liberating move. But let's see the fight's evolution in their own words:

Dave: I was making waffles for breakfast, and Hildy came into the kitchen upset and wanting a fight. My wife is not a fragile woman… When she is pissed, she is scary. So she attacked [verbally], and I told her I didn't want to fight. She said she did, and then I remembered what Judith said and just looked her in the eye and hugged her. She then melted and told me she was freaking out about the house being a mess, not going on the expensive vacation, and the large amount of money we just spent on the car, and needed a cry. It was weird, but I felt joy for having the tools to handle that situation. Historically, we would have had an attachment breach, hijacked the hell out of each other, and fought in that situation.

Instead of running from the fight and hiding from his wife's anger as he usually did, Dave turned toward the fight. He recognized Hildy's pain and the upset that was underneath her anger—and wrapped her up in a hug instead. And Hildy melted in his arms, letting go of her anger, getting vulnerable, and sharing her fear, pain, and what was really going on with her. She reflected on and addressed some of her unfinished business from childhood, shed her false self, and let go into her husband's arms.

Hildy: I could feel the tension building each day as the car was costing more money and departure day for our vacation that we couldn't afford was approaching. I was irritable, snapped at my children for the smallest infraction, and wouldn't make eye contact with my husband. I avoided balancing the checkbook and threw myself into cleaning up the house. I exploded after three days of negative self-talk and silent persecution of everyone around me. I stomped downstairs to my unknowing husband and started yelling at him for not caring about our finances. He gave me a hug, and I started sobbing and was able to tell him the truth. I planned an elaborate vacation when feeling a frantic need to connect with my family. I wasn't reconciling the checkbook because I didn't want to face there was no way we would go on that crazy expensive vacation, especially with the car expenses. I also admitted that I was embarrassed that I carried the fear and anxiety in my family of origin, and I did not want to repeat the same pattern with him. I was able to cut through the rationalizations and get the release that comes with telling the truth.

Challenge Your Limiting Beliefs About Yourself

If you've been working the steps of the process and applying them to your avoidance or fights, chances are you are starting to notice patterns. Whether you are Dueling Over Dollars, stuck in Family Feuds, or engaged in any of the fight types, you'll discover similar yearnings and mistaken, limiting beliefs beneath your conflicts.

Early in our relationship, Bob would talk; I wouldn't. Frustrated, he'd yell, "Talk to me, goddamn it. Talk to me. Now!" and he pursued me as I ran from room to room, shutting the doors in his face, screaming, "Leave me alone!" He'd yell louder. I'd retreat faster. Sullen, withdrawn, angry, and upset, I'd go write in my journal. I was having an I Can't Stand the Way You _____ fight all by myself.

And then there were the times when he'd be telling stories and making points at parties or gatherings that erupted into You Embarrassed

Me fights on the ride home. One of the most intense battles occurred after he made some comments to my sister and brother-in-law. In the car, I was seething: "I can't believe you said that to them. I am so embarrassed. How could you? What makes you think they care what you think? You know, they will never tell you up front. I can just hear them gossiping and talking about you now."

I started to notice a pattern to these fights, and it wasn't all about Bob. As I looked deeper, I saw that my whole family had the same beliefs I did, that the world was a disinterested and dangerous place where good people didn't talk about themselves or challenge others. My whole family was engaged in a self-fulfilling prophecy, and Bob was breaking the rules.

I had married an opinionated man. While initially attracted and fascinated by Bob's points of view, wide-ranging curiosity, and deep insight, my fascination turned to annoyance and judgment at his seeming arrogance, strong opinions, and verbal banter, and to the dissing that would erupt into I Can't Stand the Way You_____ fights.

I finally realized that what was really bugging me was that, unlike Bob, I wasn't used to being listened to and wouldn't think of stating my opinions so forthrightly or feel that entitled to state my thoughts. I couldn't imagine expecting to be listened to, let alone being respected for my opinions. My mistaken belief was that I didn't matter and that no one would really see me or get me, unless it involved work or a program I was leading. And I resented and judged him for expressing his opinions and expecting to be heard. I was projecting my denied self and my opinionated stance onto Bob, and I resented him for it. Revealing this to myself was easier than acknowledging it to Bob; I preferred my self-righteousness to getting vulnerable and letting him off the hook.

Instead of getting stuck in this stance, I developed my ability to voice my own opinions and expected to be listened to. I needed to shift my mistaken belief about not being seen or heard. How could I be heard if I didn't speak up!

I began liberating even more by pushing myself out of my comfort zone and systematically asserting myself, voicing my opinions, disagreeing, speaking up, and recognizing when I felt hurt or wanted to hurt back. I began to realize that I could assert myself rather than fight. I began to stretch myself even further, speaking up more and demanding to be listened to.

As we developed, not only did we fight less, but Bob often conceded points to me. This really reinforced my liberating. I realized that I now expected to be listened to. I was completing unfinished business: from feeling like a ghost child growing up, not being seen consistently, existing in isolation, to being seen, heard, connected, and having influence. Perhaps even more surprising to me was that the more I expressed myself, the less arrogant I found Bob to be! We still fight, but now we are most likely to have flash fights that are quickly resolved and end in better decisions, both for us and for our work.

We suspect you have similar stories about limiting beliefs to the one Judith just related. Reflect on what they are and what you need to do about them in order to liberate. If you're unsure how to free yourself, read on.

Change Beliefs with Vision and Following Through

Changing your limiting beliefs isn't a simple matter of saying or thinking a positive thought. Liberating is something you do, not just think about. It takes repeated action, behaving as if you believed the empowering belief. Give yourself daily life assignments to challenge limiting beliefs and develop new thinking, acting, and feeling patterns—what we call the assignment way of living (Wright and Wright 2012).

We're not talking about doing positive affirmations (they don't work). Instead, we're encouraging you to act in ways that are consistent with these empowering beliefs (which does work). It works even better if you take the time to envision the new behavior: "If this happens, I will do that." The more of these contingencies you envision, the better (Wiseman 2013).

Liberating means trying out new behaviors that are consistent with new, empowering beliefs about yourself. You may not believe it initially, but if you give yourself the benefit of the doubt and try to embrace and act on an empowering belief as if you believe it, you'll find that it becomes a new belief. If you feel that you don't matter, for example, and you act as if you were someone who did matter or who was loveable—you are more likely to change and become that person (Wiseman 2013).

Act on Empowering Beliefs with Liberating Assignments

1. Pick a limiting belief that you discovered in revealing (for example, I'm not enough; I don't matter).

2. What empowering beliefs do you want to live by in its place? To help you choose more empowering beliefs to live by, see which of the following resonate with you:

Mistaken Belief	Empowering Belief
I'm too much.	My feelings and thoughts are valid.
I don't matter.	I matter.
I'm not loveable.	I am loveable (for who I am; I don't have to earn love).
The world is a hostile place.	The world is supportive, and others want the best for me.
There's not enough for me.	There are sufficient resources (time, money, love, energy).
I'm not enough.	I am sufficient.
I am a burden.	I am a blessing.

3. Specify actions you're going to take that implement the new belief that should also challenge your mistaken belief. For

example, ask yourself: If I believed that I matter, how would I act, what would my posture be like, and what might I do or say? Now choose an action you will experiment with such as

- ask for what I want at least once a day;
- experiment with following a yearning at least once an hour;
- stand and walk with pride;
- express my opinion and preferences five times a day, including what we have for dinner and where we go on dates;
- write down the significant contributions I make each day and the positive things my partner does for me as evidence that I matter.

4. Now, implement the actions. Act as if you were someone who believed these new empowering beliefs every day, or several times a day. Keep conscious that this is what you are focusing on. Remember, the steps you take don't have to be big. In fact, small is better—it is frequency and consistency that matter. Keep stretching. Add exercises from the rest of the chapter.

5. Journal on how you feel after taking action.

Challenge Your Beliefs, Get to the Heart of the Matter

So far, we've focused on *beliefs about yourself* that have been playing out in your fights and your relationship, but now it's time to challenge your *beliefs about relationships*. Liberating is breaking out of this cage of limiting beliefs as well. And when you do, you'll experience more of what makes you and your partner tick and become closer—and less of what ticks you off and leads to distance and dissatisfaction.

What ticks couples off?	What makes couples tick?
Being bored	Novelty
The same old fights over and over again	Liberating into new ways of being and behaving
Being careful, manipulative	Being real, expressive
Sameness, frustration, not changing or growing, hopeless about things changing	Exciting encounters Adventures of intimacy
Not being affirmed or not having influence	Affirming, celebrating, and empowering each other
Seemingly endless power struggles	Sharing power and decision making, great teamwork

We're all under the influence of the limiting beliefs of an old model of relationships, a model that's all about preserving the status quo, championing those who don't rock the boat, don't get angry, don't fight, and just try to get along. But the old model doesn't work to improve relationships or yourself; it keeps couples stuck and prevents them from evolving into intimate partnerships. The old model stems from deep unconscious attitudes that see individuals and relationships as fragile rather than resilient and capable of growth.

Each of us needs to develop our new model for fighting and relating with fresh empowering rules that challenge and grow you and your relationship. We know liberating goes against the old rules that are so familiar—that's the point. And because these new ways of relating may seem uncomfortable and unfamiliar, you may start to doubt yourself and wonder why you are stirring things up, picking fights, taking risks, and blurting out truths. Breaking rules, no matter how limiting, goes against our unconscious tendency to avoid risk. Remember, you are breaking the rules for a reason: to have the best relationship you possibly can and to become the best person you can be. To back up your new moves, we want to share what we've found in our couples work and what the research shows that makes for creative fights and great relationships.

Liberating Moves: Take Action to Break Your Old Rules for Relationship

The old rule is to be careful. But if you treat yourself and your relationship as a hothouse flower, you won't bloom under the conditions of real life and true love. Alternatively, test your relationship and fight full-out following the rules of engagement (name-calling is against the rules), and you and your relationship will become more resilient. Following are powerful liberating actions to break old limiting relationship rules, build a new model of relating, and take the relationship to a new level.

Identify Your Fear and Rock the Boat

Where have you been afraid or reluctant to rock the boat in your relationship? Settled for less than you want because you've been afraid to stir things up? What have you been holding back on? Think about ways you try to keep things on an even keel, to not make waves and challenge your relationship. Let your yearnings guide you. Don't like how you spend your evenings, dates, money, or time? Want something more in your spiritual, sex, or family life? Broach the issue. Talk about it.

Be Real, Not Careful

Genuine interaction means you're spontaneous, unedited, and real, rather than carefully choosing your words. It also means you're more likely to start a fight. But that's the point—being yourself with each other and bringing conflict to the surface so you can deal with it. Real intimacy requires vulnerability and deep truth. Identify where you tiptoe around, afraid of making your partner unhappy, upset, or mad. Are you waiting until he's in a good mood before you broach a topic, sugarcoating your point, buttering him up? Don't want to "ruin" a good time by bringing up a tough topic? Stop it. You're partners; you're in this together. Treat each other with kid gloves, and you'll never really touch each other.

Inventory where you are manipulating or managing your partner, practicing what you're going to say before you say it, fudging the truth, holding back, and so forth. Get real. If you're upset, show it. If you need something, ask for it. If you have a thought you would normally edit, say it. A feeling unexpressed? Share it. Speak up!

Say what you think and feel, share your opinions, fight for what matters, express your feelings—yes, we mean all of them. Be forceful, be expressed! If you make a habit of speaking up when things bug you, you won't build up resentments and withheld communications that come blurting out in crazy-ass fights, or result in cold détentes that combust when you least expect it. You'll more easily find satisfying solutions and clear the air.

At the end of the day, scan for unexpressed communications, withholds, and resentments—uncommunicated feelings, thoughts, judgments, even gratitude, love, or compliments. Check your gut. Were you hurt or angry and didn't express it? Held back your thoughts, feelings, or judgments? Your care, love, appreciation, or gratitude? Keep track, and now, go share it.

Talk About the Big Stuff Daily

It's not just talking—it's *what* you're talking about that makes a difference in relationships. Most couples think they are communicating with one another, but they are mostly handling logistics and dealing with to-do's.

Thriving couples talk about more than what's for dinner, who's picking up the kids, or the plans for the weekend. They talk about the big stuff—their feelings during the day, hopes, fears, and dreams. They create a sense of shared purpose and meaning in their relationship beyond tasks (Gottman 1994). They keep getting to know each other, not just in the beginning stages of the relationship (Miller 2013).

Schedule one nonlogistical talk daily; even fifteen minutes can make a big difference, and you may be surprised to discover how few nonlogistical conversations you are having. Every day at a mutually agreed upon time, ask each other things like, What's on your heart and mind? What's going well? Where are you struggling? What are you afraid of? What do you yearn for? What are you looking forward to?

What are you feeling? What were your hopes today? Your dreams? How are you living toward your vision today?

Keep Current

"It doesn't matter… It's no big deal… He's busy… I shouldn't bother him." Forget the belief that things—or you—don't matter. When you are up to date, backlogs of judgments and upsets are less likely to come blurting out in an ugly fight. Don't wait to share until your partner is in a good mood or keep things to yourself because you judge them to be unimportant. Recognize that you are partners and that you need to keep each other informed about your lives and feelings as well as "fessing up" to your upsets and resentments.

Have a weekly date and hold it sacrosanct. And don't just plop in front of a video; make time to talk.

Make a habit of daily sessions where each of you speaks while the other listens without interrupting for a few minutes so that you can both express fully what you are feeling and thinking. It's like thinking and feeling out loud—you often don't know what you are upset about until you start to flow. Having that space to speak and listen to one another really deepens your understanding and intimacy.

Fight Early and Often

Forget the belief that things will just go away. Don't let fights fester. They only get messier and harder to unpack. When you start getting annoyed or dissatisfied, it's time to talk about it. Remember, if you sweep it under the carpet, you'll only trip on it later and cause more harm. The happiest couples fight early and often (McNulty and Russell 2010). Tough, honest, angry fights are more helpful in the long run than bottling up your upsets. Fighting when an issue arises makes it much easier to handle. By fighting early and often, conflict becomes more "normal" in your relationship so it's not such a big deal when it happens. Haven't had a fight this week? You're getting behind.

Sweat the Small Stuff

Everything matters. Contrary to another author's advice, you should sweat the small stuff—don't let it build up to big stuff. Satisfied couples address the bumps in the road rather than create detours around them (Orbuch 2009). Fears and worries loom larger and surface more when you aren't communicating and let things build up (Levine and Heller 2010). Look for the small stuff that is bugging you—don't ignore or dismiss it. Deal with problems on a granular level before they become oversized and complex.

At the end of every day (or bare minimum, once a week), do a scan. Have you been annoyed? Irritated? Vaguely dissatisfied? Hurt? Angry? Dismissing your feelings like it's no big deal? What's the issue? What's bugging you? Deal in. Discuss it with your partner. Make a Saturday breakfast ritual to fill in the blanks: What I appreciate about you and our relationship this week is… What's been bugging me is…

Pick a Fight!

Why wait for explosions? Picking a fight when you are not all charged up, when you are not already in the heat of things, can be really productive. It teases issues up to the surface that need tending to.

Use the rules of engagement, the right side of the engagement continuum, and all the tips of liberating. Do a deep dive into the issues yourself even before you broach them with your partner. What is really bugging you? What do you yearn for? What are you feeling? What do you truly want? What are your mistaken beliefs that are playing out in the issue? Now share all this with your partner.

If you are the one who is blaming or sticking it to your partner in the Blame Game or Hidden Middle Finger gambits, tell the deeper truth about what is going on with you and say more directly what you want and need. Picking a fight consciously, rather than waiting for it to surface in the heat of a moment, can be a liberating and powerful experience.

Review the list of fights, pick one, and go at it:

1. The Blame Game

2. Up and Down Toilet Seats and Other Domestic Disputes

3. Dueling Over Dollars

4. The Hidden Middle Finger

5. Sexual Dissatisfaction

6. If You Really Loved Me, You'd…

7. I Can't Stand the Way You…

8. You Love _____ More than Me

9. Family Feuds

10. Told-You-So's

11. You Always _____, You Never _____

12. Deception Perceptions

13. You're Just Like Your Mother/Father

14. You've Changed/You Won't Change

15. You Embarrassed Me

Shake It Up, Baby! The Importance of Novelty and Excitement

Liberating means freeing yourself from old patterns, breaking free from ruts and routines. So, shake it up. Grow. Change. Do new things. Fight to bring the thrill to your relationship—make conscious, concerted efforts to introduce novelty, surprise, and variety. Too many couples settle into boring routines, which is deadly to relationships (Tsapelas, Aron, and Orbuch, 2009). Couples who keep learning, growing, and changing have exciting, satisfying, close relationships.

Make your dates count. Exciting dates are better than pleasant ones (Aron et al. 2000, Lyubomirsky 2013). Go deep. Have a "challenge date" at least once a month. Challenge each other—discuss issues outside the relationship and make observations about how each of you is generating problems for yourself at work, with friends, or in other areas outside the couple relationship. Support each other to keep learning and growing to be your best. Have "show-and-tell" and "inspiration" dates regularly where each of you brings new ideas, demonstrates a new skill, and shares what you are learning and what inspires you.

Set and Keep Your Standards High

People think they are helping when they tell you: "You expect too much from your relationship. You're going to be disappointed. Lower your standards." Bad advice. Really bad advice. Want good advice? Don't settle. Expect a lot from your partner and your relationship. Liberating means you make your own rules, set your own standards, and set them high.

Keeping high standards helps you break free from mistaken beliefs, like the belief that you don't matter or you're not worthy, or that the world or your partner won't support you. Act as if you expect communication and passion. Hold that standard, don't settle—and you are more likely to have the relationship you yearn for. Couples with idealistic standards tend to have relationships that live up to those standards (Baucom et al. 1996).

Yes, having high standards may spark some disagreements. You may engage in Blame Game conflicts because you accuse her of sabotaging your social life with her television addiction. You may start some Told-You-So fights because you predicted his apathy about his job would prevent him from getting the promotion that at one point seemed a certainty. These high standards, though, are good fight catalysts, pushing the relationship forward rather than allowing it to languish.

Our couples create a powerful vision for their relationship and develop mutually agreed upon standards and operating agreements to back it up and live it. This helps them move through fights more readily.

They pick standards that they won't deviate from in diverse areas, including house maintenance, daily chores, finances, socializing, and daily interactions. These can be simple household standards such as dishes are done before we go to bed and we greet each other warmly—we stop what we are doing and greet each other like excited puppies. Having standards reduces a lot of unnecessary conflict—couples agree ahead of time on how best to do things—and it brings a greater sense of security, teamwork, and intimacy. They resolve fights by creating new standards and operating agreements for the future.

During the first ten years Judith and I were married, I was running a fast-growing, multifaceted business with my business partner, and I had a two-year waiting list for accepting new private clients. I was excited and stressed and noticed that when I came home from work, I wanted Judith to leave me alone. It occurred to me that I was treating her worse than my clients. That was really bizarre, since she was more important to my happiness than they were. I changed and immediately established standards for my entry—greeting her warmly, asking how her day was, and really listening while sharing my daily experiences, and doing something together. I began looking forward to seeing her when I got home. Home became a place for even more warmth and sharing. Today, almost three decades later, homecoming is still a delight.

Become an Intimate Team—Join the Couples' Olympics

Question your belief that sex is intimacy. While sex can be a great way to express intimacy, it's rarely the best way to create intimacy. What if life together were foreplay? Couples battling to bliss experience deep intimacy from teamwork and partnership. We learned this the hard way.

We'd planned a couples' workshop to focus on joy and intimacy, with exercises to foster affection and closeness. We figured that it would be an enjoyable, warm, laughter-filled weekend. What we found? Joy and affection wasn't something you could "paste" on top of whatever was going on with the couples underneath. When we got real, we found these couples were clashing: struggling with priorities; arguing about messy basements; disagreeing about parenting; feuding about money, undone tasks, and territory battles. They were struggling with the "stuff" of living together, learning to cooperate, getting things done, handling chores. These patterns spark a lot of fights, unnecessary squabbling, or hostile distance, and they were wasting a lot of time and energy.

We tried another tactic. When we asked the couples when they had experienced closeness and intimacy with others in their past, it was when they'd been part of a sports team, a musical group, or worked together on a project. We then shifted the focus of our couples' program to the "couples Olympics," helping them become life teams who loved working and being together. Each couple picked a project with challenging outcomes at our monthly seminars and then competed with other couples the next month with ratings for difficulty, importance, creativity, and degree of partnership.

The more teamwork they demonstrated, the more intimacy they experienced. They had more fun, meaning, affection, appreciation, and trust and expanded their expectations of each other. Now, they were experiencing joy and intimacy! It wasn't about romance per se but getting things done as a powerful team, loving the experience, and stretching themselves and each other!

Make your couple a powerful team and experience the intimacy it creates. Pick a project to work on together every month. Make a game out of how you can clean the kitchen together, organize the basement, or beautify a room. Decide your rating criteria: efficiency, fun factor, and creativity, for example, and score yourself from 1 to 10 like the Olympics. Give yourself a time limit and go for it. Recruit other couples to compete with you in the couples Olympics to spur you on.

Share Power and Follow the Highest Denominator

Be great partners beyond the bedroom, and you'll experience more love and satisfaction. In the happiest relationships, partners respect each other and share power and decision making. He's secure enough to let you influence him and isn't into just getting his way to assert power and position, and if he's not, there's an 81 percent chance of divorce or the relationship collapsing (Gottman 1999)! Sharing power means empowering each other. When that happens, we recognize each other's superior competence and values in some areas and not only defer, but enthusiastically support the other's initiatives. We call this following the *highest denominator*.

Having a fight about chores, money, or how to do, handle, or accomplish something? Assess who has the higher standard or is the more skilled, and follow the highest denominator. Good teams know the strengths and weaknesses of all the players. Suss out your relative strengths, and you'll avoid a lot of unnecessary fights, learn to respect each other's gifts, and learn from each other.

Continual Investment, Priceless Rewards

If you aren't willing to become who you could become or if you're failing to use your relationship as a transformative vehicle, you are missing out. Liberating is an ongoing way of life, not a singular moment of freedom. We've seen inspiring transformation in couples as they continue to liberate throughout the stages of their marriages—from having kids to empty nesting and beyond. They don't settle; they keep exploring the boundaries of their relationship. That doesn't mean they don't get stuck sometimes, or coast, or backslide, but they get back on course.

They don't bicker and battle for the hell of it. They do it purposefully, recognizing that out of the conflict, powerful emotional expression, and tension comes something stronger. In the middle of a heated debate about who is being selfish, it might not seem like a liberating moment. Cumulatively, however, these debates open up the relationship to mutual insights and growth, providing the energy for couples to push themselves and the relationship forward.

While we are encouraging you to be strategic in liberating, we mean it in the way that Abraham Maslow (1994) meant it when he talked about extended, self-induced peak experiences that characterized self-actualized people. Peak experiences didn't just "happen" for them. They required a lifetime of long and hard effort, setting up the conditions whereby peak experiences were more likely to occur. Liberating consistently helps set up the conditions for free expression that facilitate these transcendent moments.

We're not just interested in helping you get along with each other; we want you to discover the thrill of living free, creating deep connection for the purpose of becoming something much greater for yourself, your partner, and the world around you. Make liberating a way of life and learn to do it strategically, and you will be learning the next bliss skill, *rematrixing*.

CHAPTER 8

Rematrix

Reprogram Your Mind, Transform Your Relationship

*R*ematrixing, the fifth bliss skill, means changing your mind—literally. You build new neural pathways of beliefs and behaviors—changing the way you love and the way you fight. It means learning to quarrel with a new and improved consciousness. And when you do, your relationship conflicts produce lasting change or even transformation. By rewiring your brain, you create new, empowering matrix beliefs about yourself and your relationship. You begin to live the new paradigm of love, where the purpose of the couple is to bring out the best in both of you.

Rematrixing means adding to and repeating the moves you make in liberating with resolve. You experimented with breaking out of your mistaken beliefs in liberating, and now you are consistently working with intent to live a new way. But the exciting moves of liberating won't last unless you do them consistently and repeatedly—this is the point of rematrixing. Without the discipline in rematrixing, you might improve your relationship, but it will drift back to what it was before or even become worse than it was previously. Or your partner may be making all kinds of positive changes, but it doesn't make much difference to you because you are still seeing her or him through the lens of your old matrix. You are filtering your partner's changes to "match" your beliefs, causing you to not see or to dismiss these positive behaviors.

That's why you must practice rematrixing repeatedly to create new empowering beliefs, behaviors, and ways of being. In fact, some of the best moments for rematrixing are when you're fighting. Fights provide optimal opportunities for brain-changing. This is when the unfinished business of your matrix is surfacing and can be addressed. Your fights then become an integrated part of the process of transformation. Your relationship arguments cease to be something to resolve, get over, or prevent—they become the catalyst for an evolving relationship.

With rematrixing, you consciously grow yourself up, take on your unfinished business, fight more productively, and love more powerfully. When you become someone you hadn't even imagined before, your relationship transforms. Through rematrixing, you take charge and become the architect of your relationship and your life.

The Magic of Rematrixing: Reprogram Yourself and Your Relationship

With rematrixing, you learn to take advantage of your brain's neuroplasticity—the ability to build new neural circuits of beliefs, behaviors, and relating that create a new you and relationship. Neuroscientists have found that the brain's ability to grow new nerve cells, forge plastic change, and acquire new beliefs and skills requires certain conditions: highly focused attention, novelty, stretching into new skills a bit outside our comfort zone, and repeating new behaviors (Schwartz and Begley 2003; Berns 2005). Yearning, engaging, revealing, and liberating facilitate all these conditions.

Most people prefer relationships to be automatic and nice, but it's the opposite that makes for great relationships. You need to learn to be conscious about everything—from beliefs about yourself to why you're fighting. When you rematrix, nothing is automatic and nice initially. Gradually, however, your relationship becomes a platform for growth and transformation—and for ever-deepening love and intimacy.

Rematrixing represents a paradigm shift: it's staying conscious in your relationship, being aware of opportunities to shift your belief system and change your behavior. Rather than just thinking about the relationship when a problem arises, you're thinking about it deeply all the time. No longer will you engage in fights reflexively and thought-lessly. Now your intent is to rematrix.

What ticks couples off?	What makes couples tick?
Making one or two moves, then backsliding	Consistently and repeatedly making liberating moves for lasting change
Getting through, getting over, or preventing arguments	Using fights to consistently change your brain and beliefs
Avoiding core issues underneath conflict	Addressing unfinished business that comes up
Only thinking about the relationship when there are problems	Thinking about your relationship consistently and deeply
Focusing on one big insight or good move and then plateauing	Constant stretching to create new, empowering beliefs and relationship

There's No Such Thing as a Quick Fix

When you understand how the brain works, you realize there is no such thing as a quick fix. Lasting change requires rematrixing—repeated, conscious stretching into new beliefs and behaviors, not just an exciting insight or a good move on your or your partner's part. This is why so many couples give up when things don't seem to be working. They go to a couples' retreat, and the relationship improves, but then they back-slide. John does what Jill has been asking him to do for months, but then John reverts to his old ways, and Jill becomes disgusted with him and the relationship. Jill and John don't understand that it's not hope-less; they just haven't understood what it really takes to change.

You've probably run across the notion that it takes 10,000 hours to develop mastery, whether becoming a prizewinning golfer, tennis champ, chess whiz, or musical genius (Ericsson 2006). That's what it takes to become really proficient in any skill. It's the same thing in relationships. But this isn't bad news; you'll easily spend 10,000 hours with your mate. It's how you spend those hours that count.

You need to spend that time on rematrixing in order to meet the conditions for lasting change—building new mental maps with deep, intentional practice that keeps these fresh neural pathways open and developing and renews your relationship.

Beware of the Tenacious Matrix

Your existing matrix is powerful for a reason; you've probably invested 10,000 hours in limiting beliefs and unproductive and reactive fight patterns. The more you think limiting thoughts and engage in reactive patterns, the more you strengthen the neural nets of those thoughts and behaviors. So you need to consistently break these old patterns and build new ones. Unfortunately, when you start experiencing new, empowering states, you "miss" the old feeling state (Dispenza 2007). As a result, you unconsciously think a stinking thought (distorted thinking from your matrix), triggering that familiar negative state associated with the mood of the disempowering belief.

The old matrix doesn't go away, and without constant rematrixing, it will reassert itself and return you to behaviors, thoughts, and feelings you assumed you had left behind. There's only so much neural real estate, and when we don't keep practicing the new behaviors, old habits move back into the neural neighborhood. We have to use it or lose it—literally.

The power of the old matrix can also derail positive changes that are happening in your relationship. Your partner could bathe you in love and never argue with you, but you still won't feel loved if you are filtering these experiences through your old matrix of not believing you are loveable or believing that you can't trust people. You'll find a way to dismiss the positive actions, not notice them, explain them away, or diminish their value.

Bob is very affectionate and acknowledging to me and often says positive, encouraging, and loving things. But because of my old matrix of limiting beliefs (not expecting to be seen and appreciated), I often dismissed his comments or didn't really register what he said to me. Now I make it a point to pay attention to his comments and to the love and care I see on his face. I consciously soak in his warm looks, his appreciation, and his loving comments. I intentionally say things to myself like, *Oh, Bob is looking at me adoringly; I am loveable.* My awareness, soaking in the positive, and turning these positive events into positive experiences have helped me build new neural circuits of empowering beliefs of *I am loveable, valuable, and worthy.*

> **Soak In the Positive**   Focus on the positive to change your matrix. Identify ways your partner shows caring and is making positive changes. Be aware of positive interactions and really experience them to help you rematrix into new empowering beliefs. Do what Judith did and consciously soak in and affirm positive interactions. Really feel them. Remind yourself that they are evidence of love and connection. Remember the first rule of engagement—accentuate the positive—and use it consciously and consistently to rematrix.

The Transformational Power of Loving and Fighting

Neuroscience research reveals exciting possibilities for relationships. Think about your neural networks of beliefs, behaviors, and ways of being and how they were originally wired through relationships with people close to you when you were a child. Neuroscientists are finding that you and your partner can rewire each other as adults in the same way (Cozolino 2014)! You redirect the implicit memories of upsets from the past and imbue each other with new memories of appreciation and understanding.

Research in the emerging field of interpersonal neurobiology explains how our relationships shape our lives and our brains—the ways the brain grows and is influenced by our personal relationships.

These studies reveal the impact relationships have on our matrix—our sense of self, beliefs, way of being, and behaving (Siegel 2012a).

Think of it this way: it's like your partner serves as an external cortex where you "borrow" his understanding, compassion, empathy, and care and wire those qualities into your brain. When you are triggered, or have an old, upsetting implicit memory surfacing, or even an explicit memory, and become aware that your partner is showing empathy and understanding, you can wire his warmth and compassion into those upsetting memories.

This is why fights are so critical for rematrixing—they are the times when our implicit memories saturate our hearts and minds. Fights activate pain, fear, hurt, and anger buried in our unconscious, our matrix of beliefs. We think we're mad because our partner is an idiot, or mean, or uncaring, and while our partner may not be a saint, we're reacting to feelings from our unconscious and filtered through the lens of our matrix.

Fights provide prime moments for rematrixing when we apply the bliss skills, become more conscious of our unfinished developmental business, and allow ourselves to experience that deep feeling. When we feel that original pain, we can share what is really going on inside of us (it wasn't about the toothpaste cap after all); that memory and the associated beliefs are available for rematrixing. When our partner is able to respond by soothing us with understanding and empathy, we can wire this empathy right into our disturbing memory. Neuroscientists have found that every time we retrieve a memory, it is encoded anew (Cozolino 2010). We don't just feel better because our partner is caring about us; we wire our partner's caring into our new matrix. This starts to change our beliefs, expectations, and way of being.

Tune In, Turn On

Rematrixing is more likely to happen when couples are tuned into their own experiences and to those of their partners. Studies show that our brains are constantly rewiring and that attuned, empathic relationships are prime avenues to rewire our circuits (Siegel 2007). Attuned means that we are aware of our own internal state and the internal world of our partner. We are mindful and not on automatic pilot. This focused attention sharpens our mind and has the power to change both of our brains (Siegel 2007).

Tuning in is facilitated by secure attachment to your partner. When you consciously work to be more accessible, responsive, and emotionally engaged, you build a foundation that makes it easier to "read" her and for her to read you. With rematrixing, you build the circuits of being there for each other, creating mutual trust (Siegel 2012b).

As you develop an earned secure attachment (Main and Goldwyn 1998), you become better at seeking support and giving it. You more easily roll with the hurts that inevitably occur in relationships and are less likely to be hostile when you are mad at your partner. Your fights shift, and you start to tune in. You and your partner become empowered—more curious and open to new information, less defended, and more open to new experience. You understand and like yourself better (Mikulincer and Shaver 2007).

But don't settle for security—use it to develop yourself by tuning in to yourself and your partner. When you're secure and tuned in, you possess a base from which to launch yourself more fully into the world, a foundation to deepen your sense of self and to stretch the relationship.

Tune In   How do you tune in? First, be aware of your own feelings, senses, and internal state. What are your bodily sensations (such as heart rate, tension, butterflies, clutch in your gut)? What emotions are you experiencing? Next, notice your partner's facial expressions, feeling states, body gestures, and tone of voice. As you focus on your experience—and on your partner's—you harness the neural circuitry of "feeling felt" by each other. This state helps you both feel vibrant, alive, understood, and at peace (Siegel 2007, 123).

When you have a sense of what your partner is experiencing, let it show. Express your understanding, care, and empathy in your eyes, face, vocal tone, touch, and gestures, as well as your words. As you each genuinely attune to the other and reveal your upsets, vulnerability, and emotions, you gradually change old wiring to new empowering patterns and an expectation of warmth and connection.

Rematrixing isn't just about being warm and understanding. It's also about being real. It's the quality of being there that counts.

Enhance Attunement When It's Easy Pay attention—especially when it's easy. When you are feeling caring, open, and available to your partner, heighten your attunement. Observe your partner's facial expressions, tone of voice, feeling state. Be aware of the deeper current underneath what your partner is sharing and respond with care and understanding. The more you practice this, the deeper the neural circuits associated with love, empathy, and compassion become.

Strive to Attune When It's Hard Reach for attunement during relationship fights. These tough moments are critically important— they offer opportunities for you to become more conscious of your internal state. Tune in to your feelings, body state, and your yearning. Don't react in reflexive, unconscious ways; follow the rules of engagement. Even if you start acting in ways that are triggered by your existing matrix, reach for attunement in those moments. The more you practice, the more you'll be able to find it.

Now let's see how an experienced couple moves from conflict to attunement on their way to rematrixing.

"Damn it! Put your frickin' cell phone down and answer me!" Charlotte screamed. "I've had it!" Locked in one of their typical You Love Your _____ More than Me fights, Charlotte was escalating a barrage of attacks and indictments directed at Connor. Besides being angry, Charlotte was frustrated by her husband's unresponsiveness. Time for attunement!

While still angry and frustrated, Charlotte started to note the hysterical edge to her voice, her shrill tone, rapid heartbeat, and escalating feelings of panic and rage. This awareness helped her become more present and attuned to herself. She named her feelings: *I'm really mad and scared. I'm flipping my lid.* This brought her frontal lobe online, rather than just her reflexive limbic system. She was still upset, but she had more presence of mind to start to reveal: *This feels so familiar—dang, this is how I felt growing up. I was desperate to get my family's attention and have them listen to me. I felt so angry, scared, and hopeless about getting any real attention from them.*

She then became more aware of Connor, who, until that moment had felt like the enemy, not her best friend and lover. She noticed the checked-out look on Connor's face that was enraging her, but then also realized that his face was pale, his breathing shallow, his eyes downcast. She started to see their familiar pattern. They had been practicing the bliss skills and knew from past fights that her hysterical tirades drove him crazy and triggered his implicit memories of being a little boy with his abusive, out-of-control mother where he'd shut down and disappear, trying to avoid triggering his mother's rages. And when he checked out, Charlotte's upset escalated.

At the same time Connor started to pay attention to his increased heart rate and the deep freeze state that he often went to when he was upset. He realized that he was angry and also scared of Charlotte's volatility. Shaking off the numbness, he noticed not just Charlotte's anger, but also the panic-stricken look on her face. She was one of six children whose parents—and siblings—often ignored and dismissed her, sending her into desperate, but ineffective, attempts to meet her yearnings to be seen and affirmed. She'd always felt that her parents loved her siblings more, and she desperately craved affirmation, but didn't get it.

With this recognition, Connor was able to trade his vision of his wife in the moment with a more appropriate one—he exchanged the harpy shrew he had been responding to for the scared little girl hungry to be acknowledged and cared about. He reached out to Charlotte, reassuring her as he shared his feelings. She apologized for her tirade and let him know the deeper feelings beneath her rant.

You have to be aware and connected to your inner world to have Charlotte and Connor's experience, which is why revealing and developing more emotional awareness and facility are so important. Implicit memories always show up as patterns—how your body moves, your thoughts and perceptions, your reflexive responses (Badenoch 2008). When you are aware of these patterns surfacing, they provide prime moments for rematrixing. You can learn to respond differently to these patterns and share your upset with your partner more vulnerably and responsibly. And when you do and are affirmed by your partner, you begin to rewire new expectations and new beliefs. And when you provide this for your partner, he or she rewires. This is the neurobiological magic of attuned connection.

From Rupture to Repair to Rapture

Connor and Charlotte were well on the way to repairing the rift from their fight. They were discovering what researchers have found—it's not the nasty words, cold shoulders, or raised voices that cause the problem in relationships. It's when you don't use those powerful moments of fights to rematrix.

It's not the fight or the rupture that matters; it's the lack of repair. And it is in the repair that we begin to rematrix, and intimacy blooms as we grow closer and closer.

It's part of being human to disrupt our connections; to say stupid things, lose it in the heat of our anger, misunderstand our partner; or to react in any number of not-so-hot ways. And when this happens during a fight (or when you are distancing to avoid a fight) a rupture often occurs. You experience an attachment breach, and you feel removed, isolated, contemptuous, angry, afraid, or deeply hurt (Johnson 2008).

Discounting, rationalizing, denying your responsibility in the rupture, or blaming your partner for the break intensifies its negative impact and creates further pain and distance (Siegel 2010). You may feel crappy about what you've done, or believe that you're defective somehow, which deepens the belief that there is something wrong with you. Blaming your partner reinforces your belief that you can't count on people. After a rupture, we often go on automatic pilot. The power of a rupture can also put us in a fight-flight-freeze frame of mind. This is precisely the magic moment for repairing and rematrixing.

Too often couples fail to repair the rupture in the relationship. And we don't just mean make-up sex, although that can be a great celebration after you've cleared the air and gotten closer! Couples rarely understand that the power is in repairing and strengthening the connection—not in winning, or avoiding, or simply resolving the issue that led to the fight. Repair done well strengthens the couple—and each other.

A repair is performed when you acknowledge the rupture and make an effort to reconnect to yourself and your partner—you remember your yearning, use the rules of engagement, reveal what's really going on beneath the surface, and make new moves to liberate and rematrix.

Once the ugly words have been spoken, or the cold shoulder is shown, you not only can repair the relationship, but also build a new matrix of beliefs and behaviors. Remember, love is messy, and the messiness of a fight brings out unfinished business from the past. This is the stuff that needs to be rematrixed.

No matter what the argument was about or how heated it became, you can achieve a great relationship if you repair the rupture. Research shows that great mothers are out of attunement with their babies 70 percent of the time! What makes them great mothers? They repair the rupture—they readjust, reattune, and make loving connections after they've been disconnected (Tronick and Cohn 1989). The same is true for loving couples—when you do, these moments can become some of your closest and most intimate times.

You don't have to wait for your partner; either of you can initiate a repair, and you can even repair yourself. Reclaiming your projections, recognizing your unfinished business, and having compassion for what is coming up inside of you creates self-repair. Repair is always available; it's a mindful way of being (Siegel 2012b).

Repair the Rupture First, acknowledge the rift. Don't ignore it. Don't blame it on your partner either. No defensiveness. Attune to yourself, and acknowledge your reactive state, your feelings, your body sensations—and label them. Attune to your partner— remember, this is someone you love and want to reconnect with. Now use your bliss skills. Identify what you yearn for, apply the rules of engagement, and take responsibility. Apologize sincerely for irresponsible behavior and express your desire to reconnect. Don't eat shit or grovel; just acknowledge your truth. Use revealing to uncover and share what's going on deep inside, what you are feeling and yearning for, and what triggered your outburst. Share vulnerably and openly. Take these actions over and over, and in this way, you'll start the rematrixing process.

Love doesn't mean that we are always close and connected. We get attuned, misattuned, and reattuned in the dance of intimacy. "Love is a constant process of tuning in, connecting, missing and misreading cues, disconnecting, repairing, and finding deeper connection. It is a dance of meeting and parting and finding each other again, minute by minute and day by day" (Johnson 2013, 26).

A Rematrixing Couple

Repairing the rupture is a crucial rematrixing catalyst, but rematrixing doesn't happen—or become an ongoing process—through repair alone. Transformative change requires many battles and other tasks that keep your neural pathways active and growing, transforming you, your partner, and your relationship!

Remember, the purpose of rematrixing is to use your fights and your relationship to build a new matrix encoded with empowering beliefs and ways of being that help you transform. We'd like to share the story of a rematrixing couple. Connie and Ed learned to relate consciously. In doing so, they became aware of the patterns that their existing matrixes spawned and chose to establish new, more productive patterns. In the process, they triggered neurological changes that changed their beliefs.

Connie started catching her patterns that often played out in Told-You-So fights—revealing, liberating, and consciously working to change her habitual patterns through rematrixing tactics and strategies. Here is a typical interaction for Ed and Connie before rematrixing:

Connie: I told you that if we took this road, we'd run into traffic.

Ed: I told you that if we would have left a half hour earlier, we wouldn't be running late.

Connie: Oh, so now it's my fault that we took a stupid route.

Ed: It's your fault that we're late.

Connie: I told you not to take this route.

Ed: Oh, yeah, like you know everything, like you're just so much smarter than me; like you always are right.

Cold sarcasm dripped from their Told-You-So's, and this fight didn't lead to anywhere but distance and contempt. The truth is that everyone makes bad decisions and no one wants to be reminded of them in a sneering tone, but Connie and Ed kept getting stuck in these snarky arguments.

Connie came from a chaotic family with alcoholic parents who were usually one step away from the bill collectors. She was the youngest of five children, feeling one-down to her older siblings and her rich friends (Connie's family was an exception in their wealthy hometown). She tried to act like she belonged and had it together but struggled most of her life trying to figure out how to do things, how to dress, how to act to fit in. She never felt secure or as if she'd made it. She had what Alfred Adler (2009) would call an inferiority complex, trying to overcompensate by acting cool and above it all. This persona helped cover up how insecure she felt inside, how she was often scrambling trying to figure out what to do, say, or how to be. She often lied to cover up (which led to Deception Perception fights).

Ed came from an upper-middle-class family with divorced parents. While he had material security, he didn't have emotional security. His alcoholic, philandering dad was distant and demanding, and his mom was self-centered and unavailable. He covered up his insecurity with a cocky demeanor, a "nothing bothers me" front, and a smug tone.

Connie was intimidated by and felt inferior to Ed's classy family and manners. Connie competed with Ed constantly on things in which he was actually superior. Underneath was an insecure little girl, scrambling to try to look like she wasn't.

Connie began revealing her pattern of interaction. She saw the deep insecurity that she was trying to cover up and the scrambling for some sense of control that came from her chaotic background. She started to share more and more of her background with Ed. As she became more vulnerable and surfaced the painful aspects of her childhood, Ed held her with compassion and understanding. Aware of what it takes to rematrix, she consciously worked to take in the kind look on Ed's face, the compassion and care in his eyes. She soaked in his care and allowed it to lessen her sense of shame at her family background and being on "the wrong side of the tracks." His acceptance helped her to accept herself. He saw her as courageous and delighted in her spunk and tenaciousness. She began to add these positive perspectives to her sense of self, consciously experiencing the empowering feelings and beliefs, deepening those neural circuits.

Ed began to get underneath his pattern of his smug, "What, me worry?" demeanor and to share with Connie his underlying insecurity and aloneness, while she provided solace and deep belief in his capacities.

With these liberating and rematrixing moves in their relationship, Connie began to see how deeply engrained her matrix beliefs were and how they kept playing out. She realized that her way of being was an addictive pattern. She was so used to feeling one-down and crappy inside that when she didn't feel that way, she'd pick a fight with Ed to bring back that familiar neurochemical wash of shame and self-pity. And the more she puffed up, the more Ed puffed up. Either one could trigger the superior "I told you so" response in the other. Connie kept focusing her attention on her internal state, watching for her inferiority thoughts and feelings. When she felt that mood state starting, she quickly shifted. As soon as she caught a stinking thought about her value, she shifted, knowing that neuroplasticity works both ways.

She used her conscious mind to program her unconscious mind: *If I start to spiral down, I will stop and shift if I can, or reach out for support if I am having trouble.... If I start playing Told-You-So with Ed, I will exaggerate it to an absurd degree until we start laughing.... If Ed is looking at me with admiration and love, I will soak in the experience to strengthen my belief that I am loveable and valuable.*

She got to where she could change the pattern quickly so it no longer was quite so prevalent. Connie saw the power of her old matrix—she had over 10,000 hours in developing mastery in her stinking thinking and disempowering beliefs. She wasn't under any illusions that she'd never feel inferior again, but she knew what to do to keep changing it and knew that her vigilance over her self-defeating thoughts is one of the most loving things she can do for herself.

Ed loved the changes in her and stepped up his own game in response to Connie's changes. He shifted his "cool" matrix to becoming much more warm and available as well as naturally owning his many gifts. Ed and Connie stopped feeling fiercely competitive with each other and began acknowledging each other's gifts. They used their Told-You-So fights to help them assess their relative strengths and weaknesses and to improve their teamwork and their relationship.

Ed and Connie learned to use the highest denominator skill and acknowledge who does what well and who doesn't. They still debate who is the better cook and who is better able to handle their finances, but they use these debates to learn from one another and be their best and grow (rather than put each other down to boost self-esteem).

They discovered the profound gift of rematrixing—the deep, intimate journey of growing themselves, each other, and their relationship.

Rematrixing Tactics

Want to do what Ed and Connie are doing? Rematrixing, and the intimacy it brings, didn't just "happen" for them. They consistently planned and implemented strategic liberating moves to meet their yearning and build empowering beliefs and behaviors. One powerful tool Connie used was developing "implementation intentions" (Gollwitzer and Sheeran 2006).

She anticipated opportunities, problems, and circumstances for rematrixing. She actually thought to herself, *If Ed kisses me, I will steep in it and tell myself I am lovable, and really feel it.* She planned her response to Ed being late: *If Ed is late, I will hug him first, then tell him I missed him. I will then ask how to avoid it in the future.*

Studies show that when you use the if-then format to spell out in advance what you're going to do when or under what circumstances, you are much more likely to put your intention into action. Pick cues that are linked to the responses you want to have, using this format: if X happens, then I will do Y. For example:

- If I am angry and triggered in an amygdala hijack with my partner, then I will call a time-out and identify what I am yearning for and look at what I was triggered by.

- If it's Wednesday night, then I will have a date night with my honey.

- If my partner is showing me positive attention, then I will notice it and soak it in, using it as evidence that I am loveable and valuable.

- If I am feeling loving toward my partner, then I will be affectionate and hug her or express it in some other way.

- If my partner is sharing something with me, then I will attune to him and consciously note what he is feeling and thinking and let him know what I heard or saw.

- If I am not feeling loving toward my partner, then I will look at what is bothering me and share it with my partner or ask directly for what I need or yearn for.

Plan If-Thens and Practice Them   Implementation Intentions can be developed systematically as part of your overall rematrixing plan. As you plan, it helps to think of situations, times, conditions, locations, and experiences where you can practice your new empowering beliefs and behaviors. Use the if-then format to make your plan to tie the new beliefs and behaviors to situations that are already occurring or likely to occur. You'll be using your conscious mind to program your unconscious mind. Now, act on them. Review your progress weekly and tweak and update your plan from your experience. Enroll your partner to support you. Better yet, work on your rematrixing plans together.

If the work of rematrixing starts to feel overwhelming, remember, skills build over time with practice. And the rewards of rematrixing are well worth it—growing intimacy, greater partnership, shared direction, and deeper love for you and your partner. Rematrixing is fueled by your yearnings—to love and be loved, to be close, to be valued, to matter, to become who you can become. Rematrixing helps you plan and strategize to identify your yearnings, engage to meet them, reveal the beliefs that are in the way of satisfying your yearnings, and liberate consistently into new, more empowering and loving ways of being.

Rematrixing takes planning and consistent effort, but what worthy effort doesn't? We've developed many tools and resources to help with rematrixing and to guide and support you on this journey. You'll find some of these on our website, http://www.heartofthefight.com. A couple of other tactics Ed and Connie found useful are listed below for you to use when you're ready.

Begin to Map Your Future Matrix   You may find it helpful to get creative and map your matrix. You can make a symbolic representation of your limiting beliefs from the "Reveal" chapter. Some people draw a three-dimensional Tinker Toy–type matrix, others make a scene of nature, and still others create colorful PowerPoints. Now, use that visual representation to conceptualize your current matrix and envision rematrixing. Evolve the image to integrate new beliefs and discoveries from your revealing. What empowering beliefs, behaviors, and ways of being do you wish to embody as you rematrix? What actions, thoughts, and feelings would reflect the new, empowering beliefs you'd like to live and relate by? Expand your map to include your future matrix—the beliefs and behaviors you aspire to. Add your ideal beliefs, actions, feelings, and ways of being as a new structure on your map. Use a color or design that clearly indicates that this is where you are heading.

Make and Implement a Rematrixing Plan   Over time you will build your new matrix strategy with an evolving plan. You can start by asking yourself: What do I yearn for in my relationship? What is my vision for my relationship? What are the mistaken beliefs I wish to challenge as I rematrix? What empowering beliefs do I want to live from? Now, plan what you could do differently. For example, schedule weekly date nights on your calendar. Pick a strategy from the right side of the engagement continuum or a liberating tactic to practice each week and do it. Review on your weekly dates. Use the resources on our website, http://www.heartofthefight.com, to help you continue to build and implement your rematrixing plan.

The Magical Possibilities of Rematrixing

Rematrixing, when it's done right and continuously, is magical. Getting to this magical point is a result of embracing and using your bliss skills. Being aware of your and your partner's true yearnings, engaging on the right side of the continuum, and following the rules of engagement set up the conditions for safety and understanding. Through revealing, you develop the skill of attuning to yourself and to your partner, becoming aware of your matrices and how they are playing out in the relationship and each other's experiences. With liberating, you act on the awareness of revealing and start to break the grip of limiting beliefs and experimenting with possibilities.

And now with rematrixing, you are setting up the discipline to consistently challenge limiting beliefs. You are activating your neuroplasticity and engaging with your partner in a way that accelerates the rewiring process. Aware of what it takes to rematrix, you are revealing—and living—more consciously and mindfully.

In short, you're using your relationship conflicts as a catalyst to change your mind in astonishing ways, growing as individuals and as a couple because of these changes. If that's not magical, we don't know what is.

And to reap the benefits of this magical possibility, you must learn the art of *dedicating*—the focus of the next chapter.

CHAPTER 9

Dedicate

Commit to Change for the Better, Forever

*D*edicating is more than a simple promise or pledge—it's a lifetime commitment to conscious living and loving, using the bliss skills when you engage in conflict, and continually learning, growing, and transforming. Dedicating makes the difference between so-so relationships and good ones, and between good relationships and great ones. Great relationships don't come from settling. They come from dedicating to yearning, engaging, revealing, liberating, and rematrixing. With dedicating you deepen your love, intensify your intimacy, and create powerful partnerships of meaning and purpose—and live deeply ever after.

Dedicating means you are committed, as a way of life, to getting to the heart of the fights and unlocking their meaning. In dedicating mode, you no longer avoid disagreements, altercations, and upsets because you know you can work through conflict by applying the bliss skills, learning more about yourself and your partner, and growing your relationship. It is a lifelong commitment backed up by disciplines that keep you on track.

Dedicating means continually choosing challenges, individually and as a couple, to keep you stretching and growing. When you're dedicating, you learn to live purposefully as individuals, as well as a couple, changing for the better, forever. This is the power of the sixth skill, dedicating.

From Beginning to Forever

You've met Doug and Deneen in earlier chapters. Their story illustrates the importance of dedicating. Doug and Deneen fell in love in college. They found solace with each other—Doug in having a beautiful girl who cared for him and Deneen in finding a man from a solid, successful family to validate her, to help her forget her underperforming father and to escape the deadness of what she referred to as her depressed family. They both yearned to be accepted and appreciated and believed they'd found "the one" to provide it.

After their college graduations, they married, and Deneen became a psychiatric technician while Doug became an analyst at a financial firm. Deneen was chronically unhappy with her bosses at the clinic where she worked, and Doug was inching along in his career as their relationship began to unravel. Deneen found life with Doug to be a bore, and Doug found her constant complaints difficult to stomach as they engaged in You've Changed fights.

As we mentioned previously, Deneen had declared she would never want to have Doug's child, and was moving out and had found an apartment. But during her individual coaching sessions with us, she agreed to give the relationship one more chance. She brought Doug in to see us, and after working with both of them, we told them our primary objective was to help them each live their best life as individuals. We exposed how each was blaming the other for unhappiness that went way beyond the marriage, Deneen with her chronic discontent and Doug for burying his head in the sand at work and home.

They were shocked to find that commitment to marriage requires that each individual commit first to taking full responsibility for his or her own happiness. They began to redefine love and unmask the happily-ever-after myth. And through revealing, they began to discover the degree to which they needed to dedicate themselves to their individual journeys and their voyage as a couple.

Doug began taking this journey seriously when he received a career setback; his bosses told him he was no longer on the partnership track. Bob helped Doug realize he needed to redefine himself and develop a vision with an overview of his profession. From this revelation, Doug began to do the work to liberate and rematrix from being an introvert with a narrow focus to becoming an extroverted visionary.

Deneen began looking at how she had always been the responsible one in her family and never had a childhood to speak of, let alone an adolescence. She became aware of her deep yearnings to live life fully, to express herself, and to be seen and known. Engaging to meet her yearnings, she began working to enjoy life more, to speak up, and to become more playful and spontaneous. Her humor began coming out at work and in her apt criticisms of Doug, criticisms that her dry, biting humor helped make palatable to him.

Through revealing, Deneen was discovering that she was not the person she had thought she was and began examining how she used her gifts to skate by at work rather than to apply herself fully and to be satisfied. She recognized that she'd been complaining about her bureaucratic bosses rather than making changes in herself and the organization. She realized she needed to redefine herself as a leader to bring about changes if she was ever to overcome her chronic discontent. Challenging her limiting beliefs about her value, she liberated by taking a leadership position in her organization's administration.

Doug began seeing the world differently as he redefined himself through revealing and liberated by becoming more social and contributing more to his clients, generating more business in the process.

As Doug and Deneen moved through the bliss process, they had more fights but used the fights to learn about themselves and each other. As they resolved their You Love _____ More than Me fights, they began supporting each other, their careers began to blossom, and they had a child. They still faced rough times as they battled over child-rearing and issues like housekeeping, but they persevered, knowing they were on a journey of redefinition and discovery.

They dedicated to bringing out their best in all areas, including earning doctorates in their respective fields, psychology and economics. Their son has matriculated successfully into college, and each of them has made still higher commitments as Doug built and sold a company to a larger firm to focus on his professional thought leadership, and Deneen pursues her next career step as a consulting psychologist.

Changing Your Definition of Love to Dedication

Like Doug and Deneen, you must reorient from cultural myths about marriage and dedicate yourself to a mutual journey of learning, growing, and transformation.

Dedication deepens your love. With dedication, you move from passionate love to companionate love (Sternberg 1986). Companionate love may be less intense than the passion of early infatuation, but it's tremendously powerful and deeply satisfying. It combines attachment, intimacy, and deep affection. And with continued dedication, companionate love blossoms into consummate love, what many consider to be the ultimate love (Sternberg 1986). Consummate love provides a palpable sense of bliss to which we can orient. This bliss provides a beacon to help us through the hard times. If we have reoriented our definition of love and marriage to include dedication, we can more readily accept the adventure and follow the rules of engagement to reach bliss.

Dedicating isn't just committing to the relationship. Couples sometimes commit to staying together because of constraints—on account of the children, religious mores, family pressures, or what they'd lose if they broke up (Stanley 2005). This can lead couples to stay together, but be miserable. True dedicating leads to richer relationships, with deepening trust, satisfaction, and love.

Consummate love must have two dedicated, whole, and complete human beings engaging with each other—people who have changed their definition of love and are dedicated to becoming their best selves.

What ticks couples off?	What makes couples tick?
Sliding rather than deciding	Committing to long-term, thriving relationships
Looking to the relationship to fix what you lack individually	Living purposefully as individuals as well as a couple
Wishing only for the passion that comes with early infatuation	Using dedication to create deeper love that is more powerful and satisfying
Committing to the relationship because of circumstances, constraints (religion, children, and so forth)	Dedicating to two whole, complete beings engaging with each other
Sliding into a relationship out of convenience or circumstances	Choosing deep, deliberate practice as part of a thriving relationship
Staying on the fence, scanning for better alternatives	Closing the back door and fully giving yourself to the relationship

Use It or Lose It: Frontal Lobe Living and Loving

Doug and Deneen dedicated themselves to changing individually and as a couple. As you can see from their story, it wasn't a casual or a temporary commitment. Instead, it was ongoing, intense, and mutual. Through good times and bad, through the romance and the arguments, they remained steadfast, and this resolute mindset helped them transform themselves and their relationship. Dedicating is a conscious way of living that activates and uses the power of your frontal lobe. Your frontal lobe is the seat of your intention and your will, from which you live consciously (rather than from your unconscious matrix). By strengthening your dedication and your frontal lobe, you keep your tenacious matrix from resurfacing and derailing your progress. But it takes consistent awareness and effort, as Doug and Deneen learned.

Their relationship was not an overnight success; no relationship reaches bliss in one fell swoop. Doug, for instance, made strides when he learned how to sell his financial consulting concepts and joined a boutique firm; then after celebrating and relaxing, he stopped being engaged and pushing himself and started struggling again.

Similarly, Deneen found that she had to rededicate herself repeatedly. Deneen loved gardening; it was a time to relax. Little did she know that her desire to relax in gardening was not just to relax; it was part of her matrix reemerging and her desire to escape responsibility, which came from feeling sorry for herself. There's nothing wrong with relaxing and resting, but Deneen was using gardening as a way to escape from feeling like a helpless victim at work. When she gardens today, its not to escape but to re-create herself, following her yearning to feel grounded and connected with the earth.

Our matrix is seeking to reemerge at all times, and it will succeed if we do not keep stimulating and challenging ourselves to learn and grow. In the words of world-renowned pianist, Vladimir Horowitz, "If I skip practice for one day, I notice. If I skip practice for two days, my wife notices. If I skip for three days, the world notices" (Coyle 2009, 88). This is dedication, and it's what you need to bring to your relationships.

Just as musicians lose their skills if they fail to practice and weightlifters lose their strength if they don't continue to lift, your relationship will suffer if you don't make dedicating a priority—dedicating not just to the relationship, but to being your best self, to a dynamic relationship, to growth and transformation, and to making the bliss process your way of living.

Dedicating is the antidote to your limbic system returning you to your old routines and allowing unconscious impulses to rule your behavior. More than that, it allows you to dream and to measure what you do against your dreams.

Keep Dreaming Ask yourself empowering questions to keep moving: *How can I become my best self? What am I capable of? What are the possibilities for my partner? What could our relationship be like* *in the future? What benefit can we bring each other? What benefit can we bring our world? What would it take to live these ways?* These are all questions of the frontal lobe, which loves to consider opportunities to formulate new ways of being.

Deep, Deliberate Practice

Dedicating requires making conscious decisions about who you want to be as individuals and as a couple. Once we decide, we go about becoming that person and that couple in a deliberate, committed manner. This was initially challenging for Doug and Deneen. Like so many couples today, they had slid into relationship instead of consciously deciding to commit.

"Sliding versus deciding" is the phrase Stanley (2005, 158) uses to indicate how couples engage out of convenience or momentum rather than deep, ongoing commitment. Whether it is the ticking biological clock or a lease expiring, many couples move in, live together, and marry without ever really deciding.

Doug and Deneen, too, hadn't really considered the implications of what they were doing. They learned the hard way that they had not chosen to be their best selves but had fallen for the "right person cures all" myth. It took them a while to discover they needed to reorient. They learned that there was no magic formula, but that deep, deliberate practice of the bliss skills was necessary to keep themselves moving forward. To this end they chose not only to participate in a couples group with weekly assignments but to also eventually lead couples programs that are based on the seven rules of engagement. They found that this kept them focused on their best selves; the more they helped others, the more this focus sharpened in their own relationship.

Making the bliss skills a habit requires discipline, and that means dedicating to recognizing triggers and training yourself until you automatically track back to yearnings when there is conflict. (Coaches can be useful here.) Then, you need to recognize yearnings earlier and engage more, thereby revealing—learning, sharing, and expanding your understanding while expressing more of yourself. You'll learn to develop a liberating habit, where you use your insights to do, say, feel, or think differently. This will find you rematrixing and consciously engaging in your own evolution.

Practice the Process: Battle to Bliss

Dedicating means using all the skills every time you have a fight, or when you find you are avoiding one. Use the battling to bliss template as a guide, and you will automatically be rematrixing. Rely, too, on the rules of engagement as you dedicate. Answering these questions will help you get to what is really going on and what to do about it. You'll find an online version and examples on our website, http://www. heartofthefight.com.

BATTLING TO BLISS TEMPLATE
THE FIGHT **Triggers:** What set the fight off? What fight am I avoiding? What was happening as the fight erupted? **Feelings:** How did I feel just before? What did I feel prior to and during the fight? Was there another yearning or feeling I was avoiding?
YEARN **Identify Your Yearning:** What did I really want to happen instead, and what did I think the fight would do for me? What's my deeper yearning beneath the fight? (Use the chart in chapter 4.) **Share:** Share your yearning with your partner and what you discovered that preceded the fight.
ENGAGE **Follow the Yearning:** Choose at least one of the seven rules of engagement and act on it, or choose a behavior or way of being from the right side of the continuum (chapter 5), and do it.

REVEAL

Look for Patterns: When have I felt this way before? Is there a pattern? What's familiar to me about this feeling? When did I feel this way before as a child?

Dig Deeper: What am I thinking on the surface, and what's really going on underneath? What core mistaken beliefs relate? What unfinished business got triggered? What is my unfinished business that surfaced in this fight?

Share: Share what you discovered in revealing with your partner.

LIBERATE

Think: Use your revealing to plan and make liberating moves: What can I do differently next time? Plan to do it differently next time, tell your partner what moves you intend to make, and do it.

Take Action: Action includes what you do, think, and feel. Just do it.

REMATRIX

Strategize: Plan and strategize liberating consistently to change your patterns and shift your mistaken beliefs. Envision situations and anticipate circumstances and opportunities to make rematrixing moves.

Use If-Then's or Implementation Intentions: If _____ (situation, circumstance, way of being, mood, time of day, event, with a particular person, and so on), then I will _____ .

Act: Now do what you planned, often and consistently.

Closing the Back Door

Dedicating means there's no exit, no getting out, and no staying on the fence. Entertaining thoughts like *Maybe there's somebody better out there... Should I stay or go?... I should look up my old boyfriend on Facebook... I wonder if my old girlfriend is in a relationship... Maybe he'll change; it'll get better... If he'd only...*is not closing the back door—it's leaving it wide open. Escape routes and vague wishes, fantasy conditions, *if you really loved me, you'd...*thoughts and fights drain the energy and vitality from your relationship and lead to unresolved, repeated fights that can take all sorts of forms, from the mundane Up and Down Toilet Seat variety to the more weighty Blame Game ones. Indulging vague wishes, fantasizing options, scanning for alternatives—rather than diving in where you are—is not dedicating, is not closing the back door. Dedicating means eschewing the what-ifs and focusing on relationship reality.

In the penultimate episode of the CBS series *Numbers*, Amita asks advice of Alan, her soon-to-be father-in-law, as they prepare to have him walk her down the aisle. He jokes at first, "If you want to get out of it, now is the time to run like hell." She asserts that she is serious, and he then responds: "I remember, on my wedding day, I had this thought, *What if I just walk away, stay single, live alone, take things simple and easy?* Over the years, I often thought about that other guy, that other man, on his own, free to do what he wanted, a life so simple, with a lot of fun, whereas mine, well, it got a little complicated and sometimes painful... Anyway, I never envied that other guy, not once" (Falacci and Heuton 2010). In saying this, Alan demonstrated that he understands the importance of closing the back door, in committing to a path and refusing to consider possible relationship escapes.

One type of fight that tends to accompany open back doors and avoidance of dedicating is If You Really Loved Me, You'd... This fight demands dedication of the partner but avoids it for the one demanding proof. Doug made this fight a test of Deneen's love, and it indicated his initial refusal to take the personal responsibility of dedicating. He used to harp, "If you really loved me, you'd keep house better, come home sooner, know what to buy me without me telling you, dress better, attend my work functions without me needing to pull teeth ..." There are infinite variations on this relationship fight: "If you really loved me, you'd take my side when your mother criticizes me," or "If you really loved me, you wouldn't speak that way to me."

Doug had grown up in a family where love was equated to mind reading. If someone didn't read your mind, it meant he or she didn't love you: "If I have to ask for it, it doesn't count." This misconception was one of the unconscious mistaken beliefs he needed to overcome to take responsibility for asking directly for what he wanted from Deneen.

Setting irrelevant standards or conditions for your partner to prove his love isn't dedicating. It leaves you an "out"—if he doesn't prove his love the way you want it, you don't invest or you may even leave the relationship. Dedicating is doing what you need to do to be satisfied and make the relationship work.

People keep the back door open because they fear losing their freedom and options. The opposite is the case. Closing the back door focuses our fear and our yearning and generates an increased range of behaviors. It keeps us moving forward in our lives and not second guessing ourselves. More than that, it requires that we face ourselves. By facing themselves, Doug and Deneen were forced to express elements of themselves they would have chosen to ignore. When Doug and Deneen looked forward and focused on where they were going, rather than just dwelling on past hurts, limitations, and what they didn't have, their energy went toward greater accomplishments, more productive conflict, and deeper intimacy—getting more than each ever imagined.

Scan for Your Back Doors Identify where you are not going for it 100 percent in your relationship. Are you holding back or indulging in ambivalence? Are you chronically complaining, rather than doing something to change things? Waffling? Are you engaging in what researchers call alternative monitoring (Rusbult and Buunk 1993)—thinking about other options and wondering about being with other romantic partners? These are all signs of back doors. If you answered yes to any of these questions, recognize these back doors and focus on closing them. Just imagine what you can do when you put that energy into improving your relationship skills instead.

Sealing Cracks in Closed Back Doors

Some couples don't question their choice of partners, but they may have cracks in the sealed back doors that allow vital energy to leak out. They are not dedicated, and their yearning is diverted into soft addictions, those seemingly harmless habits that can drain our life force and suck the vitality out of our relationships (Wright 2006).

> When Bill entered our program, he was a high-tech engineer addicted to gaming—leading to valid You Love Gaming More than Me fights with his wife. After six months or so of personal growth work, his wife said she finally had the man she married back. He was no longer spending four hours a night on the computer; instead he was playing with the kids and actually going to bed at the same time she did. His career took off too, and he got a raise and was once again on the fast track at his company.
>
> Bill realized that his craving for gaming was masking his deeper yearning for excitement, challenge, and sense of mastery. When he began facing the challenges in his family and his job, he discovered the excitement and closeness he'd been missing and the fulfillment of developing·mastery in the game of life, rather than simulated games.

Soft addictions, like too much television, shopping, social media, or even working out, can lead to stasis and have big costs in relationships. We numb our yearning and our feelings that could lead to productive fights and positive changes in the relationship. We fail to reactivate our prefrontal cortex. We escape from the discomfort of really being known by ourselves and our partner, focusing instead on our screens, shopping, or whatever else we do.

When we don't operate out of addiction, our yearning leads to engaging more naturally and we don't divert our yearnings into superficial wanting—draining behavior that neither moves us ahead nor nourishes us. Soft addictions serve as artificial substitutes for the intimacy and other things we really need. No matter what form your soft addictions take, it ultimately takes dedication to reestablish the deeper yearning in place of cravings and wantings.

Learn from Your Soft Addictions   Rather than leaving cracks in your back door by indulging in your soft addictions, learn from them. Be aware of your soft addictions, use them to identify what you are truly yearning for, and meet that yearning in fulfilling ways, especially with your partner. Each soft addiction is a misguided attempt to meet a deeper yearning. Translate that superficial craving to the deeper yearning underneath—and meet your yearning directly.

For instance, if you are spending more time on Facebook than face-to-face with your partner, you may be yearning for connection, for belonging, or to matter. Make sure you have a regular date time and that you are also asking for attention and connection. Reach out to your honey for a hug, for reassurance, or to share what is upsetting to you. Practice the positive and creative actions on the right side of the engagement continuum to meet your yearnings more directly. (For more tips, see Judith's book, *The Soft Addiction Solution* and visit http://www.judithwright.com/soft-addictions. You'll find an inventory to discover what your soft addictions are and a template to get to your yearnings underneath your soft addiction. Play the soft addiction game for a fun way to relate soft addictions to deeper yearning.)

Flipping On the Up

Dedicating involves different types of discipline, and one particularly valuable type is "flipping on the up": taking a risk when things are going well. Doug and Deneen learned that when things went well, they began coasting, and when they began coasting, they stopped their frontal lobe living and began regressing. Their matrix reemerged. They had ceased the discipline of engaging in constant and continual rematrixing.

When things go well, go for it. Noble Prize winners Kahneman and Tversky (1979) identified a phenomenon called *loss aversion*: the imagined pain of loss is experienced as much greater than the potential pleasure of gain in risk and doing something new. Loss aversion leads us to hang on when things are good instead of flipping on the up and investing still more, like any good athletic team does when a certain play or gambit is working. With loss aversion, we begin living our lives to avoid pain. We hold on rather than taking something good and trying to make it better.

In order to understand flipping on the up, imagine that you were in Las Vegas and you had just won a hand. Flipping on the up would mean doubling down in this case. Conversely, there are times when you are losing. In these instances, you need to walk away, pay the price, and learn the lesson. Loss aversion also explains why we hang on to bad investments.

The same thing can happen in a relationship. Doug and Deneen paid the price when they were having problems and got help. Sure, when things are going badly, get counseling; however, imagine if more people got counseling when things are going well, which is the best time, as Doug and Deneen learned.

Flip Up When things are going well, ask: *How can we make things better? How can we learn and grow even more? How can we stretch ourselves and dig even deeper to see what our relationship is capable of?* Now, act on it. Admittedly, it takes discipline to ask these questions during good times, but it's the discipline that's crucial to dedicating.

Envision Dedicating

Dedicating is facilitated by vision, giving us a sense of where we are going, a direction to orient toward like using a compass in the woods. It keeps us oriented, motivated, and committed. Vision helps us keep moving over time in a consistent way. It informs our goals and our plan to carry them out, and helps us imagine how to change course when there are obstacles. Vision is powerful and helps launch new possibilities. The fathers of the United States envisioned a democracy declaring freedom and justice for all. Parents envision wonderful futures for newborns, and fathers giving their daughters away envision wonderful lives for them.

If you've read this far, you have been developing an increasingly detailed vision of your possible relationship. We'd like to add to your vision. We envision a future for you of trust, understanding, and closeness, with warmth for nourishment and support through the hard times. We wish you appreciation and gratitude from your partner, as well as challenge and excitement, with budding possibilities on the horizon. We imagine a relationship where you both are learning, growing, and fulfilling your potential on a mutual adventure of ever-deepening intimacy and possibilities.

There is so much more to envision that resides in our hearts, and will in yours too, as you allow yourself to take what you have imagined and practiced as you have read the book. Now, it's time for you to work on your vision of a rich future together, battling to bliss, getting to the heart of fights, and sharing in joy.

> **Create a Vision**   Give form to your dedication by creating a vision for yourself and your relationship. Let your heart speak by asking yourself: *What do I yearn for in my relationship? What would my life be like if I were fulfilling my yearnings? How do I want to be? What kind of person do I envision myself becoming? How will I feel? How will I act? What will be my way of being? How will I express myself? What is possible for me and our relationship?*

Now ask these questions from a couple's perspective: *What is my vision for our relationship? For our interactions, home life, teamwork, well-being, empowerment, and use of resources? How will we be together? How will we act? What will we feel like? How will others experience us? What will our statement be to the world?* (Have your partner also answer these questions if possible.)

Now write your vision as if it were already true in the present tense: *I am... I do... We are...* Flesh out your vision with feelings, sensations, and ways of being. Don't focus on measurable goals, but on a felt sense of how you will be, feel, and act, and what and who you will be as a couple.

Courage to Love

Through dedicating and using your bliss skills, you discover the rich possibilities of intimate relationships and ever-growing love. You not only enrich your relationships, you become better and stronger as your relationship grows. But as you've discovered by now, dedicating to being your best and living your vision takes courage as well as skill and practice. Dedicating requires that you face your fears as well as embrace your joy, that you become even stronger and more loving as you create even stronger and more powerful, loving partnerships—the focus of part 3.

Open Your Heart

and Expand Your Vision

Emotional Maturity

Intimate Living, Loving, and Fighting

R eal intimacy takes courage, honesty, and emotional intelligence to know how you feel, who you are, and what you stand for. Living the skills we've discussed, you will discover that you must think clearly, courageously, and honestly while also feeling fully. This means developing emotional maturity. Without this quality, you will misunderstand intimacy, thinking that it only involves being validated and accepted.

Real intimacy is more daring and audacious. It takes dedication and frontal lobe living, with responsibility and vision. It requires that you be prepared to soothe your own hurts and fears, not just look to your partner to take care of you or to make you feel accepted and safe. It is not just being unconditionally loved: that is dependent. Self-validated intimacy, on the other hand, is a key element of this chapter—becoming your own person, differentiating from your family and your partner, and developing the emotional maturity required for deep intimacy. As you develop emotional maturity, you experience its gifts: greater emotional facility; mutual empowerment; independence; the trust of strong, maturing lovers; and deep, intimate love—the topic of this chapter.

Growing Up, Growing Together, Growing Closer

"You complete me." "I can't live without you."

Romantic? No, these famous refrains may sound romantic, but believing them means you have yet to develop your full emotional capacity for deep intimacy. If you don't feel complete in yourself and are looking for someone to complete you, you are not your own person—an independent individual who can dedicate to the demands of a mature relationship. You are not fully differentiated (Bowen 1993). That means you haven't finished growing up and leaving home. You're not a separate individual distinct from your family or your partner. You haven't yet finished your developmental process.

It takes two developed, complete selves to create intimacy. Most of us reach adulthood without developing our full self. We then unconsciously try to complete ourselves in relationships. But two undifferentiated selves result in a fusion, an enmeshment that some mistake for intimacy (Bowen 1993).

Think about it this way. What is more intimate: hugging really close where you are looking over each other's shoulders or standing with noses just six inches apart, eye-to-eye? If you are enmeshed, as in the former scenario, you can't tell where one ends and the other begins—you don't "see" each other because you are too busy compensating or hanging on, fused together. In this state, your feelings and thoughts are determined by the other. Intimacy requires that we be able to stand on our own and see each other as separate, distinct selves.

The Dynamic Drives to Be Separate and to Be Close

In all successful relationships, a dynamic tension exists based on two powerful life forces: the pull of togetherness and the push for individuality (Bowen 1993). To the extent that we harmonize these forces and get them to work together, we have satisfying lives and intimate relationships. Mature emotional development requires managing the tensions of individuality and partnership.

Fights are often unconscious attempts to deal with these forces—either pushing away to be separate or misguided attempts to get closer. One of us may be trying to get close, and the other wants distance. Some couples pick fights when they are feeling too close and it gets uncomfortable; others when they've been apart and are uncomfortable with the distance.

It takes emotional maturity to navigate these forces. We must learn to resist the temptation to be distant or to "glom on to" our partner. We must develop a mature self-identity, distinct from our family of origin. That means developing into a strong, self-aware, self-determining individual who maintains individuality while sharing openly and responsibly in a way that stimulates further development of both you and your partner. And that includes battling to bliss and getting to the heart of fights.

With this maturity you freely express who you are, your opinions, your preferences, and your desires whether your partner approves or not. As you develop and mature, you also develop emotional fitness. You have a full range of emotions for which you take responsibility. You are not threatened when your partner is growing and changing or even when your partner refuses to grow.

The more you become a distinct human being, the less anxious you are about being accepted or loved. You orient toward your yearning, not obligation, guilt, locked-in roles, or expectations. As you become more fully differentiated, you have more emotional facility and can soothe yourself in fights and upsets, rather than be frozen or freaked out.

When you are poorly differentiated, you have either firm or nebulous expectations. When the firm ones are not met, you become upset, stuck, or inflexible. When the nebulous ones don't come to focus, you feel lost and can be moody. With either pattern, when you are disappointed even slightly, relationship tension builds and can often erupt in fights. Since differentiation begins with distinguishing yourself from your family of origin, these tensions often erupt in Family Feud fights like the following young couple at the beginning of their bliss journey.

Family Feud—From Daddy's Little Girl to Her Own Woman

Jamie and her husband, Eric, were accomplished professionals and active socially. They appeared strong and independent. They seemed like the last couple who would engage in never-ending Family Feud fights.

Eric: Stop calling your mother every time you're upset! Which is like every day! You're a grown woman for God's sake. And I've had it with all the time we spend with your family. I've had it! I'm your family now! And I expect you to act like it.

Jamie: I can't abandon my family. It would kill them if I told them we didn't want to go to their house for dinner every Sunday. What would they think? I can't hurt their feelings. I'm their daughter!

Eric: You're my wife, dammit!

Jamie expected little from Eric other than familial compliance. She was struggling to please her husband and please her family, never really looking at what would please her. Jamie was unable to dedicate to the relationship, and she was enmeshed with her family of origin. Her fights with Eric and his firm expectations were deeply disturbing, but she also wasn't willing to dismiss her family's expectations.

Jamie was not a distinct, developed individual. Stuck in family roles, her main identity was as her parents' daughter and not as her own woman or a wife. As a result, Jamie believed that Eric was being mean. She couldn't understand how he could demand that she not spend time with her family or look to her mother for daily advice. Whenever Jamie found herself caught between Eric and her family, she heeded the voice of whoever was the most upset or disapproving.

Jamie sought support, and as her growth group challenged her, she began to realize the costs of her family enmeshment. She was limiting her growth and preventing herself from experiencing the intimacy she yearned for and the freedom to be herself.

Jamie saw that she was being driven by fear of her family's reactions to saying no to them and being judged a "bad" girl. Once she examined these issues, Jamie grasped that she was really angry that they demanded such allegiance and that their love was conditional on her compliance.

As she dug deeper, she realized that she was afraid that she would no longer be daddy's little girl; she also worried about the fights her father and mother would have if she were not there to act as a buffer for them on holidays and other occasions. Jamie was more invested in avoiding fights between her mother and father than avoiding fights between herself and her husband, and she came to understand that Eric was correct when he complained that she refused to grow up and leave home. Using the rules of engagement, she realized how much she blamed Eric for her feelings and how difficult it was for her to take 100 percent responsibility for her own satisfaction, since she constantly looked to others to see if she was okay.

Jamie reoriented and began to use her fights with Eric to recognize stuck points in her development and was determined to change the pattern. As Jamie and Eric used their bliss skills, they tapped their deeper yearning and Jamie began to look at what she desired, rather than just what her family or others wanted. She discovered how much she was acting out of guilt, not desire, and that she didn't really want to spend so much time with her family either. They both realized that the path to more intimacy wasn't so much to work on the relationship, but to work on themselves—for each of them to develop emotional responsibility and complete their unfinished business. They were on the way to rematrixing their own values, beliefs, and standards.

Initially, it looked like Eric was the more independent one; the reality was that both Jamie and Eric were at about the same level of differentiation with the same degree of selfhood. This is usually the case—we select partners at about the same level of differentiation or sense of self (Schnarch 2009). Eric had a cooler, aloof, "I've got it handled" presence, but this false self covered up his own limited emotional range and inflexible roles and opinions. He had more distance from his family, but hadn't completed developing himself either, and self-validated intimacy was equally unavailable to him.

Eric and Jamie were getting more honest with themselves. You can too. Check yourself out: Do you call your family out of guilt or obligation? Would you avoid seeing them if there weren't repercussions? Or, is much of your social life spent with your family? Are your family members your best friends? On the other hand, do you assiduously avoid your family because of the discomfort, fights, or someone else in the family with whom you have conflict? In either case, you have got work to do to become your own person and have the foundation for mature intimacy, which is self-validated intimacy. That means being emotionally aware and following the rules of engagement, especially taking 100 percent responsibility for your satisfaction.

The more you follow the bliss skills—yearning, engaging, revealing (your unfinished business, false self, attachment patterns, mistaken beliefs of your matrix, and relationship triggers), liberating into new behaviors, and rematrixing into a genuine self—the more you will develop emotional range, flexibility, and responsibility. And as you do, you become more differentiated and capable of greater intimacy.

You will come to understand this important truth about successful relationships:

> *The best relationships aren't when you work on the "relationship"— it's when you work on yourself.* (Gilbert 1992)

Intimacy Is an Inside Job

By individuating and differentiating, Jamie and Eric developed emotional separateness and emotional maturity. You can achieve the same goal. If you have a clear sense of yourself in an intimate relationship, you discover and develop, rather than lose yourself.

By establishing self-boundaries, following your yearnings, and aligning to your vision and values, you develop a sense of equality with your partner, not a score sheet, but a stance you both assume. You each accept the other as talented, responsible, and free. You respect each other. You are open and direct in all your communications.

In this way, you are able to achieve self-validated intimacy as opposed to other-validated intimacy (Schnarch 2009). To help you keep this distinction in mind, consider how each type of intimacy is articulated.

Other-Validated Intimacy: "I'll tell you about myself, but only if you then tell me about yourself. If you don't, I won't either. But I want to, so you have to. I'll go first, and then you'll be obligated to disclose—it's only fair. And if I go first, you have to make me feel secure. I need to be able to *trust* you!"

Self-Validated Intimacy involves providing support for yourself while letting yourself be known: "I don't expect you to agree with me; you weren't put on the face of the earth to validate and reinforce me. But I want you to love me—and you can't really do that if you don't know me. I don't want your rejection—but I must face that possibility if I'm ever to feel accepted or secure with you. It's time to show myself to you and confront my separateness and mortality. One day when we are no longer together on this earth, I want to know you *knew* me" (Schnarch 2009, 107).

Intimacy, Differentiation, and Emotional Maturity

Self-validated intimacy only happens when you are an emotionally mature, differentiated individual. To experience self-validated intimacy, you need to develop a strong sense of yourself and become increasingly emotionally mature. To the degree that you can say that you have a clear sense of who you are in intimate relationships, know what you believe and value, and don't defend your false self, you will find that you can better keep a sense of perspective of both your own limitations, anxieties, and shortcomings as well as your partner's. You will blame less and engage more in facing yourself, standing up to your fears, and confronting your dark side (e.g., selfishness, hatred, manipulation, withholding, sadism, self-denigrating).

As you work to individuate and differentiate, you will fight a lot less to avoid yourself and more honest conversations will ensue. Your partner may be surprised as you admit when you are wrong even when it is not reciprocated. As you cop to your projections and distortions, you will become more relaxed with yourself and you will more easily accept the pains of growth, realizing that if there's no pain, there's no gain. As you relax with your own limitations, you will more quickly mobilize yourself outside the relationship too and move more consistently toward yearning-based aspirations. You will better support and soothe yourself in times of challenge and cut down on compensatory indulgences like soft addictions. You will also berate yourself and your partner less and choose self-validated intimacy over other-validated intimacy.

Remember, no one is mature all the time. Being real is the point. Maturing emotionally and becoming a full self is a lifelong endeavor.

Rate Your Degree of Differentiation   Consider the qualities of emotionally mature, differentiated individuals in relationship as described in the section above. How differentiated are you? Rate yourself on a scale of 1 to 10.

10 = You have a clear, strong, undefended, yearning-based sense of self and the courage to take stands, admit and accept your dark side, and show emotional maturity and self-validated intimacy in almost all circumstances, even under pressure.

1 = You are prone to blaming, projecting, enmeshment, being fear driven, being flooded with emotions, and other-validated intimacy, especially in tense or conflictual situations, and may even avoid knowing and developing yourself.

Only by orienting toward greater differentiation will you experience the bliss that's possible in your relationship and in life.

Emotional Maturity Facilitates Real Intimacy

Jamie still feared reactions of her family, but she did not let that stop her, and she buckled under to Eric a lot less. She was learning to use these moments marked by strong emotions as opportunities to develop—a requirement for intimacy. At times she even told Eric and her parents of her fear, and she was surprised to notice herself getting angry at their reactions. She was expressing and discovering the inherent power of her emotions.

Jamie was becoming her own person, capable of all these behaviors and more. Using the bliss skills, she was becoming emotionally mature, experiencing the power of her emotions and how it helps us increase intimacy.

Being emotionally mature means that you are aware of your feeling states, sensations, and bodily experiences. You use the wisdom of your emotions to guide you. Your feelings are how you sense your yearning and the nudges of your urges, and emotional awareness triggers the insight of revealing. Developing your emotional facility helps you liberate and face the fears of busting limiting beliefs.

You won't transform to your fullest or have the most fulfilling relationship without facility in the whole range of emotions. Becoming deeply aware of and skilled in your emotions is different from controlling them. In fact, control of feelings is the major barrier to emotional intelligence and intimacy. Most people seek to minimize fear and anger. That is like putting magnificent stallions in a tiny stall and trying to keep them from running free. We expend inordinate energy repressing feelings rather than learning to recognize and express them to advantage—fulfilling their natural functions.

Jamie was experiencing herself and her feelings like she never had before. She felt as if the life force was flowing more freely through her. She became more spontaneous, fluid, genuine, and alive—and more of her own unique, distinct self. Jamie was discovering a secret of intimacy: the more she became her own person and the more she developed her emotional fluidity, facility, and maturity, the more intimacy she experienced. She realized that her relationship to herself and her emotions was what led to experiencing deep connection and closeness, that it wasn't dependent upon just her interactions with Eric.

When an orchestra performs a soul-stirring symphony, it is because each musician knows and is playing his or her unique part. Similarly, only lovers who know and express themselves freely and fully are capable of deep intimacy and partnership.

And, just as an expert musician learns the notes of the scale to read music and practices to perform beautifully, lovers must learn the ABCs of love in order to create lasting, durable, intimate relationship magic. Musicians playing together must be able to read each other and coordinate their play. Lovers, too, must work to understand each other at the highest level in order to harmonize their relationship. They learn and master the language of the heart—the focus of the next chapter.

CHAPTER 11

Intimate Intelligence
The ABCs of Emotional Literacy

Great lovers read and respond to each other at a very high level—their feelings, motivations, values, desires, and much more. They flow from intense challenge to tender embrace with ease, reading each other and expressing themselves effectively. They may be masters of the emotional vocabulary but they are always learning new subtleties of expression and understanding. Ablaze with anger or humming with hurt, they mute intensity when needed and explode into expression when desirable.

Their inner awareness comes from self-knowledge and vigilance while their understanding of their beloved stems from attentive sensing and genuine interest. These lovers breathe the breath of sweetness and radiate adoration. They never stop learning the language of love and seeking to express and understand more each day. They continually develop their emotional awareness, facility, expression, and maturity.

They never abandon the basics, expanding their expression and understanding with attention to the building blocks that help them learn from pain and enhance pleasure. They hold themselves accountable to speak love clearly, be it in joy, hurt, or anger. They seek clarity and deepening contact.

They develop fluency in the language of emotions—the language of the heart—and increase their intimate intelligence with practice and expression.

Primary and Secondary Emotional Education

To learn a language means that we learn the basics, consistently build our vocabulary, and practice communicating and expressing to develop greater facility. Learning the language of love means that we continually develop our emotional intelligence to deepen our intimacy.

We all have the primary emotions of fear, hurt, anger, sadness, and joy, but we need to become more conscious of them and feel them more deeply if we want to battle to bliss.

Secondary emotions combine primary feelings. Guilt is one example: it combines hurt, fear, and often anger. Your guilt may not look like fear, hurt, or anger at first glance, but it usually contains these three in some proportion. Secondary emotions are experienced differently by different people because they are based on our personal internal experience base, which combines primary emotions in unique ways (Damasio 2005). The primary emotions are like the alphabet, and the secondary emotions are like words combining these. For our purposes, we'll work to master the alphabet.

Most people have some level of mistaken, negative beliefs about emotions—that there are "good" ones like joy and "bad" ones like fear, anger, hurt, and sadness. Joy is even suspect in some dour families. Properly deployed for their natural, intended function, *all* feelings are good—they are powerful aspects of the human experience, each encoded to anticipate our needs and prepare us to act to diminish hurt or danger and experience greater pleasure. It's not our feelings that are bad; it's our lack of skill in being with them and expressing them responsibly that causes problems.

My Attitude Toward My Feelings Notice your emotions during the day. You are having them all the time, but most of us are in the habit of noticing only the more extreme ones. What judgments do you have about emotions or feelings? Which emotions do you feel okay expressing, and which do you judge as bad, and suppress? With which ones are you most comfortable? Do you judge fear to the point that you don't even recognize it when you are holding back, nervous, or hesitant? Do you suppress hurt because it is not "adult" or manly? Do you sit on anger because you believe it only makes messes? Are you good at embracing sadness? Is joy dangerous? Learning to recognize and negotiate emotions effectively will help you realize there is no such thing as a bad emotion, just the ones we are afraid of and have not learned to use.

Primary emotions have a basic purpose: to lead us from pain to pleasure. For example, fear leads us to safety, hurt causes us to seek healing affirmation, and anger gets us away from hurtful or fearful situations and toward desired outcomes. Sadness results from lost pleasure or love, and it facilitates mourning. Joy is pure pleasure; it fuels expression, interaction, and enthusiasm for possibilities. When these emotion-specific resources are unlocked, we experience a sense of energy and vitality, broader awareness, openness, and a sense of well-being (Fosha 2000).

When we share emotional experiences with our partner and "feel felt" (Siegel 2010, 189), we fulfill our yearning to be understood and known. We don't just feel better through sharing and connecting this way; we are *becoming* better. Jamie discovered that while she yearned for Eric's approval and enjoyed feeling felt, she was able to self-validate and maintain an equilibrium that was formerly unavailable to her. She began to express her feelings even in the face of disapproval.

Developing emotional maturity enhances self-validated intimacy, and the deepening intimacy matures us emotionally. Being able to effectively deal with regulating and expressing your emotions in the face of conflict, anger, shaming, or disapproval indicates self-validated intimacy. In mature relationships, you can have different opinions and values from your family members and your partner, and you can still stay emotionally connected to them. In an intimate, committed relationship, this allows you to be known and to fully know and love another.

Assess Your Emotional Facility and Intimacy Skills   Assess the emotional skills and capacities you'll need to develop emotional maturity and self-validated intimacy.

Are you able to stay in a conversation with your parents and family—or your partner—when they disapprove? Can you disagree with them and stay even-keeled or at least engaged without withdrawing or blowing up? How do you handle their guilt trips: Do you comply, shrink away, or feel the need to blame or guilt trip back? Do you cave in to relationship pressures or others' desires? Or are you reactive against others' wishes? Can you reject others' opinions or desires without being hostile or passively disconnected? Can you belong and still be fully yourself?

The Four Directions of Emotional Facility: In, Out, Up, Down

What exactly are emotional skills? Too often, couples think emotional facility is only toning feelings down, numbing them, or making them go away. This is, perhaps, a useful tactic if you're in a business meeting or approaching a total meltdown, but emotional skills should also include the ability to rev up—increase your emotional idle so you can engage more quickly, intensify your joy, or activate your anger to make the changes you yearn for. The more you are open to your emotions, the easier you can express and regulate them appropriately (Cozolino 2010).

Jamie knew she was afraid of displeasing Eric and her parents, but she did not know how to recognize her hurt or anger, and expressing these feelings took even more practice. Shy as Jamie was, she was more emotionally aware than Eric. He found it difficult to recognize any emotions.

These emotional abilities include being aware of how an emotion affects your body, naming what you are feeling, expressing your emotions fully and responsibly, and allowing the emotion to fulfill its function. We refer to this last ability as completing the emotion. This includes being able to comfort yourself, using anger to get rid of pain, grieving loss, facing fears, releasing sadness, and taking the risk of reaching out to share pain and joy with partners and others.

Because developing emotional facility is essential for intimate relationships, we'd like to share a framework that will help you achieve this goal. Eric and Jamie were identifying emotions when they learned to understand how to up- and down-regulate, to express what they felt, and to take in objectively what the other felt. They found our model of the four directions of emotional facility—in, out, up, down (Wright and Wright 2013)—to be very helpful as they developed emotional facility.

THE FOUR DIRECTIONS OF EMOTIONAL FACILITY

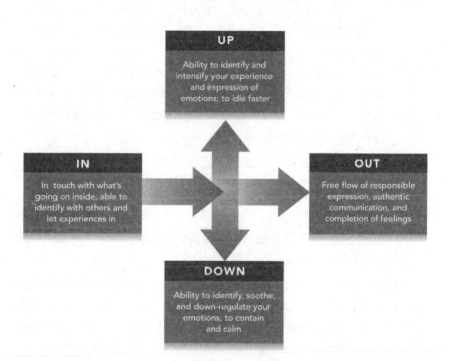

- *In.* Being in touch, knowing what's going on inside of you and what you are feeling. Perceiving your sensations, being aware of your emotions in the moment, letting experiences in. Understanding yourself and your partner. Being sensitive to events and to your internal experience. You are able to sense, feel, and name your emotions, which helps you be aware of your yearning and experience full aliveness and empathy.

- *Out.* Free flow of responsible expression. Fully expressing your feelings and allowing them to complete themselves. Not hysterical dumping, but responsibly communicating and expressing emotions in a way that brings you into greater accord with yourself and your partner. Authentically expressing your emotions, being fully present, with a full range of responsible feeling available, from crying to belly laughing.

- *Up.* Increasing your affect or intensity in expression or reception. We often think of this as being upbeat. Being aware of your present state and able to increase your awareness of, and intensify, your emotions—experience your feelings deeply, experience your joy more fully, engage more quickly. It's key to motivation and taking action, like having a faster idle so you can take off quickly.

- *Down.* Having the capacity to soothe, calm, and modulate intensity—contain (not suppress) your emotions when you are overwhelmed, or when you are prone to being irresponsible about their expression, or when you've "flipped your lid" (Siegel 2010, 22) and lost your higher-level functioning and need to regain your composure.

Remember, no one has the perfect mix of all four elements—we can always develop more facility no matter how good our emotional intelligence (EI) is to begin with. If you're like Jamie, you are good at in and down but need to develop more up and out. Eric worked to become good at out and up and now is working on down.

Assess the Four Directions Review your days for clues to assess your facility in the four directions. *In:* Were there times you were out of touch with what you were feeling and needed to develop more awareness? *Out:* Do you think you need to be expressing your emotions more? *Down:* Are there times you think you should have expressed less or not been so charged up? *Up:* Were there times where you were slow to act or it took you too long to move or engage? Where do you need to develop more of your emotional facility—in, out, up, or down?

Exploring In

Not sure what's going on with you or what you are feeling, or even if you are having some emotions? Pay attention to sensations in your body. Notice your moods, thoughts, and behaviors. These give you important clues to unrecognized or repressed feelings. You are learning to look inward. When you learn to pay attention to these sensations in your body and become more aware of your moods, thoughts, and behavior, you're more likely to recognize the related emotions.

Become an Emotional Detective   Scan for emotional clues in your body, moods and thoughts, and behaviors:

Body Sensations: Do you have a tense jaw, sweaty palms, rapid heartbeat, butterflies in your stomach, heavy chest, knot in your throat, shallow breathing, clutched gut, tense sphincter, or clenched fists?

Moods and Thoughts: Are you tense, defensive, critical, shy, sarcastic, aggressive, judgmental, cranky, moody, or in the grips of "poor me"?

Behaviors: Are you overeating, lost in Facebook, procrastinating, or indulging in other soft addictions?

These are indications that you're covering up and numbing feelings. Name your primary feeling—fear, hurt, anger, sadness, joy—to help break the spell.

Monitor a Feeling an Hour   Set a timer to go off every hour. When it goes off, close your eyes, discern the primary feeling you are having at that moment, and then immediately write it down. You may be surprised at how they vary as you develop your emotional awareness.

Coming Out

Suppressing feelings comes at a great cost. By trying to keep your feelings under wraps, you drain critical cognitive resources—it degrades your memory and your ability to think and make decisions (Gross 2002). Inhibiting your feelings doesn't make you feel better; it interferes with your ability to cope and use your emotions effectively. To the extent that you block one feeling, you block them all—your joy and your love are suppressed. Neuroscience research finds that is far better to acknowledge and express your feelings and to use the other bliss skills to integrate them.

Lieberman and colleagues' studies (2007) show that naming what you're feeling calms your amygdala and brings the conscious, visionary thinking of your frontal lobe—your prefrontal cortex—back online. You still are in touch with the feeling, but now you can apply the bliss skills, think more clearly, and act more effectively on the feeling.

Share your feelings with your partner as well as with others you trust. This engages the speech centers of your brain too, which adds to the effect. These emotional expressions may feel awkward until you build the words or synonyms into your active vocabulary. You can also write your feelings in a journal or compose a poem, especially longhand, to help tame your feelings and bring more resources to your prefrontal cortex.

Express, Don't Suppress Name it to tame it. Label and express your emotions—fear, hurt, anger, sadness, joy. When these feelings arise, say, "I'm angry," or, "I'm hurt." This simple yet powerful technique calms your aroused amygdala and brings your higher-level thinking back on board.

Play the Feelings Game Practice identifying your emotions regularly to be emotionally fit and more ready to interact in a fight or conflict. Do an emotional inventory each day. Couples we coach often use dinnertime to share one event from the day that evoked each of the primary emotions from fear to hurt and anger, sadness, and joy: "Today I felt sad about my assistant announcing he was taking another job after being with me for eight years." Keep going until each of you has named something for each of the primary emotions: "I was sad/angry/afraid/hurt/happy about _____ today." Journaling works too.

Getting It Up—So to Speak

Up-regulate to experience your feelings more deeply, amplify your emotional experience, and rev up your engine to engage in life more fully. Intensify your joy. This keeps you from ruminating, or dwelling in negative thinking. It is not indulgence or getting an ungrounded "high." It's fully feeling your emotions so they can guide you to right action. When you are having joyous feelings, you savor them and strengthen their impact. And when you are "blah," low-energy, or disengaged, you spur yourself into action.

> **"Get It Up"** Notice when you have low energy or are in a down mood and need to motivate yourself—and up-regulate. It may be when a meeting is lagging or you're dragging your feet and know you should mover faster and be more engaged. Up-regulating requires that you be able to shift a mood. See if you can "get it up." Can you generate excitement when you are feeling down?

Calm Down: Dealing with Arousal

When you're furiously angry and loaded for bear, scared and ready to head to the hills, or agitated and crawling out of your skin, chances are your fight-flight-freeze response is triggered. You are in a high physiological arousal state and need to bring some higher-level functioning online. It's time for the down skills of emotional facility. We're not talking about shutting down, numbing, or suppressing your feelings. Down-regulating means that you are able to focus and act consciously.

We all need a certain amount of stress and arousal to activate our neuroplasticity, which is one of the many reasons that fighting is good for us. Too little stress or arousal and our brain isn't triggered to wake up and rewire. We need states of moderate arousal—combined with the balancing power of nurture—to maximize the ability of our networks to process and integrate information (Cozolino 2006).

Yet, too much arousal and our brains are flooded; we're in an amygdala hijack, and we've flipped our lid and lost our higher-level functioning. We're in fight-flight-freeze mode, and either emotional extreme isn't good for relationship conflict.

In order to diminish these immediate reactions of fight, flight, or freeze, you need to learn how to deal with this rapid onset of arousal and choose another path. Remember, in these situations you are likely to start seeing your partner as an enemy or predator, rather than as your lover and best friend. This state is responsible for a lot of those destructive behaviors on the left side of the engagement continuum and the ruptures that occur when you fight openly or punish each other with withdrawal.

We're not letting you off the hook here—you can't escape the costly relationship repercussions by claiming "My amygdala made me do it." But you do need to develop strategies that deal with your arousal and bring your higher-level functioning back online, activating your frontal lobe's executive thinking center to process the emotions and sort through how to handle these situations or impulses from the amygdala. The point isn't to just "calm down"—it's to spotlight what's really going on with you, so this is a moment of discovery, revealing, and understanding. For the passive-aggressives among us, this means recognizing when we withdraw and owning that this is what we do when stressed. Whether you shut down or escalate, these are prime moments for rematrixing. But first, we need to down-regulate and mine the data.

Name that you are hijacked and in fight-flight-freeze mode. Your frontal lobe will come back online to help you make sense of what's happening, and you will be able to harness it for desirable outcomes. Use your bliss skills to deal with the arousal. *Identify your yearning* underneath the upset. *Use the rules of engagement* to get responsible, acknowledge, and tell the truth, and redirect your energy toward what you want to fight *for*. *Reveal* your unfinished business that just flared up. That means that you dig to understand as well as to share what you learn with your partner. As you understand and share, you *liberate* from that old pattern. You use the moment to get closer to yourself and your partner. These open moments are the best times for *rematrixing*—and the moments that will create emotional bonds and deep connection for the two of you.

> **Check Your Pulse** If your heart rate is over 100 beats per minute—and you're not in the middle of a workout—you're hijacked! Many of the nasty behaviors on the left side of the engagement continuum accelerate your heart rate, raise cortisol and stress hormones, and increase negativity. Stonewalling, criticism, defensiveness, and contempt are all likely to activate your and your partner's arousal. Use the rules of engagement. *Now!*

A hint for men from Bob: Are you stonewalling? Are you shutting down, mumbling, giving the silent treatment, muttering in a monotone, changing the subject, walking away, or zoning out? Stonewalling and withdrawing is a fight-flight-freeze mechanism. You may think you are calm, but numb is not calm. It is unconscious—you're under the influence and hijacked. Your physiology probably reached arousal prior to stonewalling—you're tuning out in an unconscious attempt to lower your arousal rate. The problem is that it not only doesn't solve anything or help you cope, but your partner's heart rate skyrockets when you stonewall! She's affected psychologically and physiologically and is likely to escalate until you explode (Gottman 1999). Studies show that when her heart rate escalates, she's likely to criticize—and, yup, you got it, you withdraw more—and you're both caught in a vicious cycle. Get out of the circle. Or call a time-out.

Time-Outs Are Not Just for Kids

There are instances when you are fighting and one or both of you is no longer rational, saying things you'll really regret later, or when you're consumed in an emotional flood and can't think straight. This is a good time to trigger a break in the action—fightus interruptus! Have a prearranged signal that stops the fight or encounter just for the time being so you can go cool off, get your head on straight, get responsible about your part of the fight, apply the rules of engagement, and work the bliss skills. Use the break to get ready to reengage, taking at least 50 percent responsibility. Think of it like the bell ringing at the end of a boxing round where you can cool down, tend to your wounds, and prepare to reengage.

Early in our relationship, Bob was a much better fighter than I was. I felt as though he had a verbal black belt and I was in the beginner's class. His words came at me rapid-fire, and I couldn't process what he was saying fast enough. I scrambled to absorb and respond. I would say our prearranged statement, "This is one of those times I need some space," and we'd stop the fight (most of the time). I'd go to another room or outside and mutter to myself how it was all his fault, he didn't understand, he's self-centered…but then, as I brought my frontal lobe back online, I'd start to see what was really going on with me, what I wanted, what I truly yearned for, and what I was feeling vulnerable about and didn't want to admit. I'd use the bliss skills and then return to the fight, much more responsible and productive, able to use the rules of engagement.

Time-outs need to have a time limit. You must reengage in the conversation within a specified time period, whether it is an hour or somewhat longer, whatever you predecide. We made twenty-four hours an outside limit. A time-out isn't an excuse to withdraw, disengage, and act like the fight didn't happen or walk away, punishing the other. It's a chance to cool down so you can have a straighter, more responsible engagement and resolve the conflict, understand each other better, and get closer.

Using Time-Outs Well   Remember in your time-out to name your feelings to tame them. This will lower your arousal and let you apply the rules of engagement. Once you've named what you're feeling—

I'm pissed; I'm scared; I'm really hurt—you soothed the arousal to a certain extent so you can think and plan how to respond.

Early Warning—Down-Regulating with Body Signals Alarm! STOP and note the sensations: *My heart is racing. I'm losing it. Yikes, I'm frozen… I can't breathe.* Now, take responsibility: *I gotta calm myself down. I need to practice my bliss skills.* Then say what you're going to do about it: *I'm calling a time-out. I'm going outside for an hour… gonna look at what the heck I am really yearning for. Why am I so triggered?* Now do it! And use the bliss skills to get underneath what's happening and lead you to new liberating patterns.

It takes a minimum of twenty minutes to calm down when you or your partner flip your lid—a perfect time to call a time-out before you return to the fight or the upsetting situation. You are attuning to yourself as you do this.

Bridging Back to Your Relationship: Reengaging, Resolving, Reconnecting

Down-regulating is a management move to allow greater connection. Once you are in touch with your yearning and the triggers of the fight, it is time to reengage and resolve. Be sure to reconnect, but, as you reengage, remember to watch for reacceleration—when the calmed-down fight picks up steam again. This often happens because you feel hurt and want affirmation, but the bliss process should help you affirm yourself. This is a time to understand your partner's point of view. When you make this effort, your partner is much more likely to listen to and affirm your point of view. Some couples apologize prematurely; this just leads to recycling the fights. Make it a point to acknowledge honestly and don't just manage your partner.

Activate Your Oxytocin—the Power of Touch

Another way in which you can engage in intimate conflict involves touching. Never underestimate the power of the human touch to help get you through the fights in ways that are productive and growth oriented. By touching, you trigger the feel-good hormone of oxytocin. It increases the sense of well-being, trust, and being calm and connected (Graham 2013).

Your body and brain read supportive touch as, "I'm here with you. I'll share the load." Touching helps the prefrontal areas of your brain that regulate emotions to relax, which frees these areas for another one of their primary purposes: problem solving (Greene and Goodrich-Dunn 2014, 14).

Keep touching, but don't stop there. Asking questions, making observations, telling the truth, being curious, and remaining open to tough conversations all activate the release of oxytocin, spreading feel-good chemicals throughout your system.

> **Risk a PDA (Public Display of Affection)**   Make a habit of touching each other warmly. Snuggle on the coach, cuddle, stroke each other's hair, touch your partner's face, sit next to each other when you're out to dinner so you can make physical contact, hold hands, put your arm around your honey, smooch often, spoon at night, go slow dancing, or whatever you enjoy together.

The Dance of Intimacy: Neural Magic of Relationship Rapport

As both of you develop your emotional facility and maturity, you deepen your dance of intimacy. You become two mature individuals, touching each other deeply, helping each other learn and grow. You both become more secure as you empower each other. Dedicating leads to the consistent emotional support and mutual emotional regulation for each of you that shifts your matrix.

As you deepen your bond, you provide emotional regulation for one another—soothing each other's upset, enhancing the joys as you celebrate each other's successes. You will deepen each other's experience of blissful moments. Not only does this feel good and bring you closer; it actually changes the structures of your brain, helping you each build new neural pathways of emotional regulation. You are helping rematrix one another, building circuits of care, compassion, and a sense of well-being.

It's not just the words you share, but your touch, tone of voice, and eye contact that help you each build the circuitry of up-down-in-out emotional facility. Repeated often enough, you can influence each other's rematrixing nonverbally. Hugs and touch comfort you. Interactions such as gentle voices or stroking hair and warm glances soothe you when you are upset and activate nonlinear, right-brain-to-right-brain circuits that help rematrix you. Just as these kinds of interactions wired your emotional circuitry as a child, you can now be rewired or rematrixed through the power of your loving relationship (Siegel 2012a).

Soothing each other—down-regulating helps you integrate your experience. When you are happy and excited and your partner celebrates with you and shares your joy, it builds your circuits of up-regulating and you experience your shared delight more fully. And when you share joyous news with your partner, you capitalize on its effects (Langston 1994)—sharing helps you savor the experience and adds to your intimacy and joy. When you are blah, nonengaged, or listless and your partner stimulates you and activates your circuitry with encouragement or challenge, it sparks you into action, up-regulating you.

As you experience these states together, your shared resonance creates greater coherence in the mind of both you and your partner. You both experience neural integration (Siegel 2006), connecting aspects of your brain that lead to well-being, empathic relatedness, and deep intimacy. The warmth and security pave the way for self-discovery; your neural nets integrate and are bathed in comfort. The dyadic emotional regulation you provide for one another flowers into the capacity for self-regulation. As you enhance each other's emotional experiences and soothe each other, it builds your ability to soothe and down-regulate yourself and to up-regulate and intensify your joy and emotional experiences. Shared resonance provides the beautiful combination of nurturance, stimulation, and challenge for optimal growth (Cozolino 2010).

This is the dance of intimacy—you experience the neural magic of deep rapport, resonance, rematrixing, and relating. Life together is a rich, stimulating, nurturing adventure. Your relationship becomes a vessel for transformation—a crucible for burning away your impurities and a womb for developing your best self—as you engage in the quest for intimacy.

CHAPTER 12

The Good Fight

An Expanding Vision of What Is Possible

Battling to bliss means that you fight the good fight, following the rules of engagement, in pursuit of your best self. The good fight of intimacy stems from yearning. It is fought during times of relationship peace and not just when we feel like we're at war. It is a discipline of tending to our yearning, engaging, and discovering. By now, you've discovered that fight isn't a bad word but describes a complex interaction that you appreciate, rather than avoid or fear. Fighting the good fight, you discover a whole new you and an intimacy and partnership beyond what you thought possible.

It is the good fight to engage in life and in your relationship fully to be responsible, to avoid unnecessary blame, and to fight *for* something, not just against your partner. You fight for the truth and to increase your ratio of creative-to-destructive interactions. You fight to reveal; to dig deep to know what is going on underneath your fights; to face the fear, hurt, anger, and sadness triggered from your past; to complete and convert them. Courageously, you reveal yourself fully, sharing with your partner. You experience the power of self-validated intimacy as you fight to liberate to risk breaking the old rules and challenge limiting beliefs about relationships. You consciously engage in your own transformation and in the transformation of your relationship. You fight to *feel* fully and to use the wisdom of your emotions to know yourself and your partner more deeply. You fight to grow yourself up to become your best self and to empower your partner to do the same. Fighting the good fight of conscious intimacy, you battle to bliss.

The Romantic Quest, the Heroes' Journey

The good fight is the stuff of heroes, who risk on a quest. The way isn't easy, but the rewards are great.

Remember the empowering definition of romance: *a spirit or feeling of adventure, excitement, the potential for heroic achievement*. Drop the romantic fairy tale of "they lived happily ever after," which doesn't lead to intimate partnerships, and accept instead the epic quest that leads to immense relational treasure. In the heroic journey of battling to bliss relationships, you explore new territories, go into the woods, cut through the brambles, fight monsters (the creatures within us), experience trials, and complete developmental tasks.

It is, after all, the stories of the heroes' and heroines' challenges on the quest that inspire us, not just their walks on the beach, moments spent reveling in the sunset, or what happens behind their bedroom doors. It is the quest that reminds us of the call to something greater, the opportunity to become something more than we have been, to discover our gifts and the gifts of our partner, to develop deep bonds.

Joseph Campbell popularized the hero's quest—the inspiration we find in mythic tales like *The Odyssey* and *Star Wars*. Couples too are inspirational and worthy of their praises being sung when they fight the good fight. They too discover a power that lies within, similar to the Greek gods in *The Odyssey* or the Force in *Star Wars*. Couples who battle to bliss discover courage, strength, understanding, empathy, and intimacy. They develop capacities beyond anything they had known before. Doug and Deneen could never have imagined what they were capable of as they began their journey from breakup to breakthrough. They empowered each other in career, in child-rearing, and in their personal development. Each earned a doctorate and became a thought leader in their respective careers with the support of their powerful partnership and deep love.

Unlike the happily-ever-after myths we debunked earlier, ennobling myths feature couples who continue to wrestle with the dark forces, fight, and struggle as they encounter barriers and obstacles, lose their faith, give up, and get up again. In the process, they develop nobly. For couples who battle to bliss, the rewards never end as the journey unfolds. As you learn the six skills, see yourself on a quest for self-validated and shared intimacy.

Accepting the Call or Clinging to the Known World

Heroes leave home willingly like Frodo with the ring or are forced to embark on their quest like Jonah and the whale. Regardless of why they depart, they discover unimagined, unsuspected worlds. As you battle to bliss, you leave your old patterns of relating and fighting, the limiting beliefs of your matrix, and outdated myths of relationship, and you discover new ways of relating and great intimacy.

Fantastic quests don't happen when you're in a rut. Many couples cling to what is familiar even if greater possibilities beckon. They rationalize: *It's not so bad… It'll get better… Maybe I should just look for someone else… If he would just change, everything would be okay… I can't stand to fight; if I just ignore it, it will go away… If we would just stop fighting, everything would be okay…*

Think about it this way: every fight is a call to adventure and to do things differently. For a graphic reminder of the call to adventure—and the refusal of the call—think about the movie *Groundhog Day*. In it, the character played by Bill Murray ignores the call repeatedly until one day he wakes up and takes on the challenges of becoming his best self and of creating an intimate relationship. The adventure is engaged, and each step leads to new territory—some pleasant and some not so enjoyable, but all part of the adventure, the invitation to new horizons.

Maybe there is a crisis in your relationship, or you see other couples living more adventurously and intimately than you, or you discover new possibilities through a book like this one. You may have taken a step to "improve" your relationship and saw that it opened up other possibilities you hadn't imagined. You then realize that there are additional options, another world of powerful partnerships. You begin to realize that the quest for intimacy and a satisfying relationship is yours to pursue and create; it doesn't just "happen." Nor is it your partner's job to make you happy and satisfied. So as you go on this journey, remember: the more you follow your yearning, the deeper you engage in your quest.

Heed the Call   What adventure of relationship is calling to you? What are you yearning for? What are the challenges that beckon? See the challenges—and your relationship ruts—as calls to adventure. Heed the call.

Braving the Woods—Encountering the Dangers and Discovering Treasures

Joseph Campbell describes the questing realm as a "fateful region of both treasure and danger" (2008, 48). The *dangers* often surface in your fights—the buried emotions and unpleasant memories you had forgotten, the mistaken beliefs and reflexive behaviors of your matrix, and the pain, rage, and fear of other unfinished business of childhood. As you face these dangers, they transmute into the *treasures* of relationship. As you meet these "dangerous" moments with the bliss skills, you see and understand yourself and your partner more clearly, experience greater empathy and compassion, and deepen your contact and closeness. These magical moments provide powerful rematrixing opportunities.

Through risking and fighting with Deneen, Doug expanded his capacities as a risk taker and truth teller. Emboldened by these experiences and Deneen's support, he risked his professional livelihood. After committing to the truth, he challenged his entire profession by sponsoring a conference with a highly respected Nobel Laureate pointing out the limitations of current economic theories in investment practices and proposing a radical change. His risk paid off, but it might not have. At the same time, Deneen was taking risks as a leader of a daring initiative in her job. They found the necessary muscle to do these things in the unlocked power of battling to bliss as they repeatedly got to the heart of the fight. They discovered the treasures of deep intimacy and partnership and greater personal and professional success.

The Road of Trials and Tests

Don't expect smooth sailing on your quest. Doug and Deneen embraced the adventure and prepared to be tested repeatedly. They had repeated trials in their relationship, professional challenges, and ordeals of parenting. As they responded to these challenges, it was impossible to imagine Deneen as the whiney victim she had been, and Doug as the distant, reserved, unengaged man that he'd been.

Each fight you engage in measures your commitment and, if the commitment is there, helps strengthens your skills. Each fight exposes your vulnerabilities and unfinished business, barriers to overcome, and lessons to be learned.

You will be tested repeatedly as tensions erupt, fights ensue, and havoc threatens. As you face your tests, remember:

- Identify your yearning.

- Engage responsibly in constructive interactions.

- Reveal your unfinished business.

- Liberate into new ways of being and fighting.

- Develop new beliefs and ways of being as you rematrix.

- Dedicate yourself.

Heroes don't pass all the tests, nor will you. It is the repeated reengagement that is crucial. The hero need not accomplish each deed or be successful at each trial, but must learn from it. Your dedication helps you glean the lessons and keeps you from allowing failure to deter you.

The Marital Arts Way of Life

Think of martial artists who stay on their feet as they deflect oncoming blows and redirect the adversarial force toward their attacker, treating their opponent with respect. As you practice the six skills of the *marital* arts, you learn to navigate the inherent tensions of relationships skillfully—to harmonize the tensions between two people with different needs, backgrounds, customs, and desires. You work to balance the contradictory drives for togetherness and for individuality, enmeshment and avoidance, intimacy and distance. The tension of these forces is often the basis of conflict, and in working with these tensions, your *marital skill* is the basis of love and connection.

Navigating the inherent tension of these forces is the hallmark of deep, loving relationships. The Chinese call the dynamic beneath these opposing forces yin and yang. And as you learn to deal with these tensions, you become more flexible. You learn to live more in the moment where joy resides. You become more of yourself, guided by the yearnings of your heart.

Marital artists are warriors of the heart. In the good fight, you battle for a cause or with guiding principles. As a warrior of the heart, you are dedicated to fulfilling your deep desire to learn and grow, to be the best person you can be. The good fight develops emotionally mature, complete individuals, who use their relationship and the impact of the other to become their best self.

Warriors of the heart are constantly conditioning, sparring, and even engaging in fights—training to keep their skills sharp and to become even more skilled at engaging in loving conflict. They know that it's not just one battle, but a campaign, so they need to keep in fighting shape and don't try to get the war over in one battle. Warriors monitor their weaknesses and work to strengthen them.

As you fight the good fight, use the mindset of a warrior of the heart by being alert for

- disempowering thoughts and beliefs from your matrix that hold you back;

- a tendency to give up or settle;

- a defensive reaction of blaming and avoiding responsibility;

- being destructive and having reactive encounters rather than exploring creative possibilities; and

- operating on the left side of the engagement continuum.

If you have moved to the destructive side or slipped into victimhood and irresponsibility, right the balance and fight the urge to blame and criticize without taking full responsibility for your experience.

Practice the disciplines of the six skills repeatedly. Evaluate your encounters frankly. Lick your wounds, restore your equilibrium, and reenter the fray, refreshed and ready for battle.

Allies Bring Out Your Best on the Quest

Heroes have allies and helpers—your partner as well as other couples who have embarked on the quest to battle to bliss can provide wise counsel. They give you the support that all successful heroes require.

Think about the allies in the historic and contemporary myths—Odysseus had Athena, and Luke Skywalker had Obi-Wan (Ben) Kenobi. They didn't go on their quests alone. Engage and find allies. At the same time, recognize and reject those people who disempower you or join you in blame and self-pity. True allies not only support you when things are tough, but they also inspire and challenge you when all is going well. Your partner can be your strongest ally. Whether you are fighting, playing, doing chores, or making love, every interaction can be an opportunity to grow and transform. Your relationship can provide the support for you to achieve your dreams.

Allies bring out the best in each other. Support your partner in the pursuit of her vision, not your vision of her but her vision of her best self. Called the Michelangelo phenomenon (Rusbult, Finkel, and Kumashiro 2009), you help sculpt your partner's ideal self. Couples who affirm each other's ideal selves not only bring out the best in their own lives, but have much more satisfying relationships as they grow toward their ideal. Every time you interact, you can be "sculpting" one another.

Allies hold a vision for one another—you appreciate your partner for who she is, but also for who she can become. You mirror the vision your partner inspires in you that is consistent with your own goals for yourself. That doesn't mean that you don't contribute to your partner's vision—you may see aspects of your partner's gifts and potential that she doesn't. It's not about changing your partner to your standards, but believing in her potential and supporting her as she moves in the direction of big dreams. We often need our loved ones and others to activate our yearning—it's hard to yearn for something if you don't even know it exists or if you have already ruled it out for yourself because of your limiting beliefs!

Bob held a vision for me of becoming an author and public speaker, getting my doctorate, cofounding a graduate university, and many other possibilities. He believed in me and saw possibilities beyond my own imagining. I hadn't allowed myself to articulate these dreams and had a much more limited view of myself than what he could see for me. His belief encouraged me to reach for the stars, when I had been limited to certain areas of achievement. For him it was no surprise when I wrote a best seller and was on *Oprah, Good Morning America,* and *20/20.* For me, it was significant rematrixing. I often fought him, resisted, balked… but was always deeply moved and excited by the vision for my dreams to be fulfilled until I could own it for myself.

The more your relationship results in you becoming a better person, the better. The more you grow, the better your relationship, because you then contribute to your partner's expanding. The more self-expansion you experience from each other—whether new ideas, different ways of being, novel experiences, perspectives, or knowledge—the more satisfied and committed you'll be in your relationship (Aron et al. 2013).

Living Deeply Ever After

What happens when you battle to bliss? What takes place inside of you and in your relationship when you fight heroically?

You experience a deep, growing love that encompasses absolutely everything in the relationship. Full of tender affection and compassion as well as challenge and criticism, your relationship is constantly growing—a thrilling adventure of partnership. You live deeply ever after.

This is where all the bliss lessons come together. This is the vision of two authentic people being themselves fully while engaged in genuine respectful partnerships and dedicated to synergizing their gifts.

The bliss process that we've described is not just about resolving fights or improving relationships. Instead, it is a template for evolving relationships beyond the traditional model. Constantly evolving couples who battle to bliss are creating new possibilities for relationships   an ever-deepening intimacy, an ever-expanding love, a never-ending adventure.

Conscious Connection to Yourself, Each Other, and the Greater World

In the journey to the heart of the fight and beyond, you, the hero, transform. You return to your everyday world with the treasure of new understanding to share. You share the rewards of your quest—the lessons of battling to bliss and the love, wisdom, freedom, or knowledge it bestows (Vogler 1998). The hero's quest does not just benefit the hero or the hero's partner; it benefits all.

As we get to the heart of the fight, we connect more deeply with one another. Not only do our hearts touch, but our minds and brains interact, creating expanded states of consciousness (Tronick et al.

1998). You experience an expansion of your consciousness that transcends the individual you knew yourself to be. This enhances your awareness, growth, and meaning, and deepens your connection with yourself and your partner.

Not only will you connect more fully to yourself and your partner, but this connection will also transfer to the world around you. The intimacy you experience will lead to a state of consciousness where you will be touching others more deeply as you are more and more engaged in all areas of your life.

You will likely see more in your everyday life and become more aware of how interconnected we are to one another—and how the connection expands to all living beings in the web of life. You will see a glimpse of connecting to the greater whole as you connect with your partner (Siegel 2010). As we experience deepening love with our partner, we begin to touch our love of humanity.

You are now on the quest for love, for ever-growing intimacy with truthful encounters and abiding passion as you work to arrive at the heart of the fight. You fight the good fight. Fight to fulfill your yearnings. Fight to reveal and discover what's really going on beneath your fights, your limiting beliefs, and the unconscious matrix that colors your world. You are learning to fight to reveal yourself to your partner—no matter what. You fight to liberate—risk, make bold moves, break out of your limits, and leap into deeper reaches of yourself for expanded intimacy. Fight to do the consistent, strategic work of rematrixing, to become your best and create alive, intimate relationships. Fight to dedicate, to consistently choose, to risk, to learn, to grow, to transform—to consciously engage in your own transformation to create an alive, growing relationship of bliss. The purpose of your relationship is now much greater as it is to bring out the best in you, your partner, and your relationship—and those you touch. You share the love so others are inspired to answer their call to the adventure and embark upon their own quest.

And as you do, imagine a world where lovers continually become more than they were through their interactions—fighting the good fight, consciously engaging in their own transformation. Imagine a world where all couples embark on the bliss journey, discovering the heart of the fight, the deep love, and sharing it with their loved ones.

Imagine a world where all relationships bring out the best in each other, where each partner develops him- or herself, contributing, bringing more into the relationship. Where each partner takes responsibility in encounters, eschews blame, and increasingly learns and applies the skills of creative, constructive interactions, and transformative encounters. Where partners know it is their job to grow themselves up, develop emotional maturity, and continually become who they can become. Where relationships are growing adventures of love and truth; honest, expressive encounters; mutual empowerment; and inspiration. Where people are real, free, with honest and genuine encounters that spark development and growth. Where fighting is purposeful—developing the emotional maturity to deal with the pain, anger, or fear that arises in close relationships and transmute it into further growth and development, understanding, compassion, and deeper love for oneself and his or her partner. Imagine children growing up in these truthful, free environments and entering their adult relationships with maturity, aliveness, and responsibility.

Imagine a world where all people fight the good fight, by embarking on the journey of honoring their yearning, engaging in transformative interactions, revealing insight into their deepest hidden areas, liberating to break free of limiting beliefs, and building a new matrix of empowering beliefs and responsible, genuine, and loving ways of being, as they dedicate to being their best, bringing their best into the relationship, and seeing the relationship as the vessel for transformative love.

This is the good fight—battling to bliss. May you be your best and bring out the best in those you touch. May you experience the deeper rewards of the intimate journey and may you share the blessing widely as you deepen your love and joy.

Acknowledgments

This has been a well-loved book, with the contribution of many loving and caring hands, hearts, and minds. With great thanks to our students, especially our Couples Empowerment Group and all of our couples groups as well as the brave souls in the Year of Transformation, Transformations Labs, Leadership Groups, and the Wright Graduate University who have been "field testing" these skills and lessons in their relationships and service.

We are blessed with a devoted staff who walk their talk and dedicate themselves to bringing out the best in themselves and all they touch. Immense gratitude to Barb Burgess, who steadfastly runs the business and does whatever it takes to get things done. Kate Holmquest has not only brought her brains, but also her heart to the game, dropping whatever she was doing to meet deadlines. Amelia Perkins has seen beauty and possibility that has encouraged us since she read the opening chapter. Rachel Zwell has been a stalwart partner with the blazing typist and editor Monica Sanden and proofreader Gloria Virtel. Sasha Sekinger and Hannah Maxwell have contributed their dynamic energy to our attraction and sales efforts; George Miller produces our blog talk radio with Stephanie Castillo, our social media manager; and Lisa Sanden has facilitated our foundation expansion. Filling in the cracks wherever needed has been our Wright Graduate University chancellor, Mike Zwell. He and all of our staff have consistently gone the extra miles to make this work. Jacky Davila has gracefully wrestled budgets while our coaches

Jillian Eichel, Gertrude Lyons, Beryl Stromsta, Karen Terry, Jennifer Stephen, Art Silver, Jon Fieldman, Dr. Marilyn Pearson (who also doubles as a trusted proofreader), and the other Year of Transformation coaches and team leaders along with our other lab leaders have all participated in the development of the materials in these pages.

Bruce Wexler insisted on this book and provided critical midwifery services, repeatedly editing chapters and encouraging us. Joelle Delbourgo, our agent, made the excellent pairing with New Harbinger. The editorial team at New Harbinger, led by acquiring editor Melissa Kirk and driven by Nicola Skidmore along with Jess Beebe and Angela Autry Gorden, gave insightful, detailed, and potent feedback. The full sales, marketing, and management teams at New Harbinger helped to get the word out about this important topic so dear to our hearts.

Quite a number of other people have given us valuable counsel, from marketing to moral support—especially Melissa Giovagnoli Wilson, Dwain Jeworski, and Dr. Robert Moore.

Special acknowledgment goes to the many relationship, neuroscience, and behavioral science researchers whom we cite for their intrepid investigation into the never-never land of truths that go against the grain but unlock the potential of us all.

Profound gratitude goes to Art Silver, John Davidoff, Rich Lyons, Scott Stephen, Stan Smith, Tom Terry, and Karen Wilson Smithbauer of the Wright Foundation for the Realization of Human Potential Board, as well as our consultant Don Delves, who not only put their money where their mouths are but where their hearts beat. Countless student leaders of SOFIA (Society of Femininity in Action) and the Men's Guild help us deliver and develop our curriculum. We are deeply grateful for your dedication and partnership.

And to all those who have contributed to our relationship, and to the great partner, we thank you.

References

Adler, Alfred. 2009. *Understanding Human Nature*. London: Oneworld Publications.

Aron, Arthur, Christina C. Norman, Elaine N. Aron, Colin McKenna, and Richard E. Heyman. 2000. "Couples Shared Participation in Novel and Arousing Activities and Experienced Relationship Quality." *Journal of Personality and Sociology* 78: 273 83.

Aron, Arthur, Gary W. Lewandowski Jr., Debra Mashek, and Elaine N. Aron. 2013. "The Self-Expansion Model of Motivation and Cognition in Close Relationships." In *The Oxford Handbook of Close Relationships*, edited by Jeffry A. Simpson and Lorne Campbell. Oxford: Oxford University Press.

Badenoch, Bonnie. 2008. *Being a Brain-Wise Therapist: A Practical Guide to Interpersonal Neurobiology*. New York: W. W. Norton & Company.

Baucom, Donald H., Norman Epstein, Anthony D. Daiuto, Robert A. Carels, Lynn A. Rankin, and Charles K. Burnett. 1996. "Cognitions in Marriage: The Relationship Between Standards and Attributions." *Journal of Family Psychology* 10 (2): 209–22.

Barry, Dave. 1989, February 19. "Blub Story a Very Deep Experience." *Miami Herald*. http://www.miamiherald.com/living/liv-columns-blogs/dave-barry/article1936692.html.

Berns, Gregory. 2005. *Satisfaction: The Science of Finding True Fulfillment*. New York: Henry Holt & Company.

Berridge, Kent C. 2009. "Wanting and Liking: Observations from the Neuroscience and Psychology Laboratory." *Inquiry* 52 (4): 378–98.

Bettelheim, Bruno. 1976. *The Uses of Enchantment: The Meaning and Importance of Fairy Tales*. New York: Vintage Books.

Birditt, Kira S., Edna Brown, Terry L. Orbuch, and Jessica M. McIlvane. 2010. "Marital Conflict Behaviors and Implications for Divorce over 16 Years." *Journal of Marriage & Family* 72: 1188–204.

Blakeslee, Sandra. 2006, January 10. "Cells that Read Minds." *New York Times.* http://www.nytimes.com/2006/01/10/science/10mirr.html?page wanted=all&_r=0.

Bowen, Murray. 1993. *Family Therapy in Clinical Practice.* New York: Jake Aronson, Inc.

Bowlby, John. 1969. *Attachment and Loss.* New York: Basic Books.

Bowlby, John. 1973. *Separation: Anxiety and Anger.* London: Hogarth Press.

Bowlby, John. 1988. *A Secure Base.* New York: Basic Books.

Campbell, Joseph. 2008. *The Hero with a Thousand Faces.* Novato, CA: New World Library.

Coan, James A. 2008. "Toward a Neuroscience of Attachment." In *Handbook of Attachment: Theory, Research, and Clinical Applications,* edited by Jude Cassidy and Phillip R. Shaver. New York: Guilford Press.

Coyle, Daniel. 2009. *The Talent Code: Greatness Isn't Born. It's Grown. Here's How.* New York: Bantam Books.

Cozolino, Louis. 2014. *The Neuroscience of Human Relationships: Attachment and the Developing Social Brain.* New York: W. W. Norton & Company.

Cozolino, Louis. 2010. *The Neuroscience of Psychotherapy: Healing the Social Brain.* New York: W. W. Norton & Company.

Damasio, Antonio. 2005. *Descartes' Error: Emotion, Reason, and the Human Brain.* New York: Random House.

Dispenza, Joe. 2007. *Evolve Your Brain: The Science of Changing Your Mind.* Deerfield Beach, FL: HCI Books.

Doidge, Norman. 2007. *The Brain That Changes Itself: Stories of Personal Triumph from the Frontiers of Brain Science.* New York: Viking Press.

Ericsson, K. Anders. 2006. "The Influence of Experience and Deliberate Practice on the Development of Superior Expert Performance." In *The Cambridge Handbook of Expertise and Expert Performance,* edited by K. Anders Ericsson, Neil Charness, Paul J. Feltovich, and Robert R. Hoffman. New York: Cambridge University Press.

Falacci, Nicolas, and Cheryl Heuton. 2010, March 12. "Cause and Effect." *NUMB3RS.* CBS.

Feeney, Brooke C. 2007. "The Dependency Paradox in Close Relationships: Accepting Dependence Promotes Independence." *Journal of Personality and Social Psychology* 92: 268–85.

Finkel, Eli J., Jeni L. Burnette, and Lauren E. Scissors. 2007. "Vengefully Ever After: Destiny Beliefs, State Attachment Anxiety, and Forgiveness." *Journal of Personality and Social Psychology* 92: 871–86.

Fisher, Helen. 2004. *Why We Love: The Nature and Chemistry of Romantic Love*. New York: Henry Holt and Company, 9.

Fosha, Diana. 2000. *The Transforming Power of Affect: A Model for Accelerated Change*. New York: Basic Books.

Gilbert, Daniel. 2007. *Stumbling on Happiness*. New York: Random House.

Gilbert, Roberta. 1992. *Extraordinary Relationships: A New Way of Thinking About Human Interactions*. Hoboken, NJ: John Wiley & Sons.

Glaser, Judith E., and Richard D. Glaser. 2014. "The Neurochemistry of Positive Comments." *Harvard Business Review HBR Blog Network*. http://blogs.hbr.org/2014/06/the-neurochemistry-of-positive-conversations/.

Goleman, Daniel. 2006. *Emotional Intelligence: Why It Can Matter More than IQ*. New York: Bantam Books.

Gollwitzer, Peter M., and Paschal Sheeran. 2006. "Implementation Intentions and Goal Achievement: A Meta-Analysis of Effects and Processes." *Advances in Experimental Social Psychology* 38: 69–119.

Gottman, John M. 1994. *Why Marriages Succeed or Fail: And How You Can Make Yours Last*. New York: Simon and Schuster.

Gottman, John M., and Nan Silver. 1999. *The Seven Principles for Making Marriage Work*. New York: Crown Publishers.

Gottman, John M., and Robert W. Levenson. 1988. "The Social Psychophysiology of Marriage." In *Perspectives on Marital Interaction*, edited by Patricia Noller and Mary Anne Fitzpatrick. Philadelphia: Multilingual Matters.

Gottman, John. 1999. *The Marriage Clinic: A Scientifically Based Marital Therapy*. New York: W. W. Norton & Company.

Gottman, John. 2012, April 28. "The Science of Trust and Betrayal." Keynote Speech. *The Couples Conference 2012 from The Milton H. Erickson Foundation, Inc.*, San Mateo, CA.

Gouin, Jean Philippe, Sue Carter, Hossein Pournajafi-Nazarlooc, Ronald Glaser, William B. Malarkey, Timothy J. Loving, Jeffrey Stowell, and Janice K. Kiecolt-Glasera. 2010. "Marital Behavior, Oxytocin, Vasopressin, and Wound Healing." *Psychoneuroendocrinology* 35: 1082–90.

Graham, Linda. 2013. *Bouncing Back: Rewiring Your Brain for Maximum Resilience and Well-Being*. Novato, CA: New World Library.

Greene, Elliot, and Barbara Goodrich-Dunn. 2014. *The Psychology of the Body*. Philadelphia: Lippincott Williams & Wilkins.

Gross, James J. 2002. "Emotion Regulation: Affective, Cognitive, and Social Consequences." *Psychophysiology* 39: 281–91.

Hahlweg, Kurt, Howard J. Markman, Franz Thurmaier, Jochen Engl, and Volker Eckert. 1998. "Prevention of Marital Distress: Results of a German Prospective Longitudinal Study." *Journal of Family Psychology* 12: 543–56.

Hanson, Rick. 2013. *Hardwiring Happiness: The New Brain Science of Contentment, Calm, and Confidence*. New York: Harmony Books.

Hart, Donna, and Robert Wald Sussman. 2005. *Man the Hunted: Primates, Predators, and Human Evolution*. Cambridge, MA: Westview Press.

Hendrix, Harville. 2007. *Getting the Love You Want: A Guide for Couples*. New York: Henry Holt & Company.

Johnson, Sue. 2008. *Hold Me Tight: Seven Conversations for a Lifetime of Love*. New York: Little, Brown & Company.

Johnson, Sue. 2013. *Love Sense: The Revolutionary New Science of Romantic Relationships*. New York: Little, Brown & Company.

Kahneman, Daniel, and Amos Tversky. 1979. "Prospect Theory: An Analysis of Decision-Making Under Risk." *Econometrica* 47: 263–92.

Karpman, Stephen. 1968. "Fairy Tales and Script Drama Analysis." *T.A. Bulletin* 7 (26): 39–43.

Knee, C. Raymond. 1998. "Implicit Theories of Relationships: Assessment and Prediction of Romantic Relationship Initiation, Coping, and Longevity." *Journal of Personality and Social Psychology* 74: 360–70.

Langston, Christopher A. 1994. "Capitalizing On and Coping With Daily-Life Events: Expressive Responses to Positive Events." *Journal of Personality and Social Psychology* 67 (6): 1112–25.

Levine, Amir, and Rachel Heller. 2010. *Attached: The New Science of Adult Attachment and How It Can Help You Find—and Keep—Love*. New York: Tarcher.

Lieberman, Matthew D. 2013. *Social: Why Our Brains Are Wired to Connect*. New York: Crown Publishers.

Lieberman, Matthew D., Naomi I. Eisenberger, Molly J. Crockett, Sabrina M. Tom, Jennifer H. Pfeifer, and Baldwon M. Way. 2007. "Putting Feelings into Words: Affect Labeling Disrupts Amygdala Activity in Response to Affective Stimuli." *Psychological Science* 18 (5): 421–28.

Lipton, Bruce. 2013. *The Honeymoon Effect: The Science of Creating Heaven on Earth*. Carlsbad, CA: Hay House.

Lockhart, Andrea. 2000. "Perceived Influence of a Disney Fairy Tale on Beliefs About Romantic Love and Marriage." Ph.D. Doctoral Dissertation California School of Professional Psychology.

Lucas, Richard E., Andrew E. Clark, Yannis Georgellis, and Ed Diener. 2003. "Reexamining Adaptation and the Set Point Model of Happiness: Reactions to Change in Marital Status." *Journal of Personality and Social Psychology* 84: 527–39.

Lyubomirsky, Sonja. 2013. *The Myths of Happiness: What Should Make You Happy, but Doesn't, What Shouldn't Make You Happy, but Does*. New York: Penguin Books.

Main, Mary, and Ruth Goldwyn. 1998. *Adult Attachment Classification System*. Unpublished manuscript. Berkeley: University of California.

Marano, Hara Estroff, and Carlin Flora. 2004, September 1. "The Truth About Compatibility." *Psychology Today*. http://www.psychologytoday .com/articles/200411/the-truth-about-compatibility.

Marazziti, Donatella, Hagop S. Akiskal, Alessandra Rossi, and Giovanni B. Cassano. 1999. "Alteration of the Platelet Serotonin Transporter in Romantic Love." *Psychological Medicine* 29: 741–45.

Marist Poll. 2011, February 10. "'It's destiny!' Most Americans Believe in Soul Mates." *Marist Poll Online*. http://maristpoll.marist.edu/210-its-destiny-most-americans-believe-in-soul-mates#sthash.BJ61NB2q.dpuf.

Markman, Howard J., Galena K. Rhoades, Scott M. Stanley, and Erica P. Ragan. 2010. "The Premarital Communication Roots of Marital Distress and Divorce: The First Five Years of Marriage." *Journal of Family Psychology* 24: 289–98.

Maslow, Abraham H. 1994. *Religions, Values, and Peak Experiences*. New York: Penguin Books.

McNulty, James, and V. Michelle Russell. 2010. "When 'Negative' Behaviors Are Positive: A Contextual Analysis of the Long-Term Effects of Problem-Solving Behaviors on Changes in Relationship Satisfaction." *Journal of Personality and Social Psychology* 98: 587–604.

Mikulincer, Mario, and Philip R. Shaver. 2007. *Attachment in Adulthood: Structure, Dynamics, and Change*. New York: Guilford Press.

Miller, Anna. 2013. "Can This Marriage Be Saved?" *American Psychological Association* 44: 42.

Moberg, Kerstin Uvna. 2003. *The Oxytocin Factor: Tapping the Hormone of Calm, Love, and Healing*. Cambridge, MA: Da Capo Press.

Norretranders, Tor. 1998. *The User Illusion: Cutting Consciousness Down to Size*. New York: Penguin.

Orbuch, Terri. 2009. *5 Simple Steps to Take Your Marriage from Good to Great*. New York: Delacorte Press.

Panksepp, Jaak. 1998. *Affective Neuroscience: The Foundations of Human and Animal Emotions*. New York: Oxford University Press.

Prigg, Mark. 2012, August 3. "Scientists Reveal the Secret to a Happy Marriage: Don't Forgive and Forget, Get Angry Instead." *Daily Mail*. http://www.dailymail.co.uk/sciencetech/article-2183169/The-secret-happy-marriage-Dont-forgive-forget-row-instead-say-researchers.html.

Rock, David, and Jeffrey Schwartz. 2006. "The Neuroscience of Leadership." *Strategy + Business Magazine* 43: 1–10.

Rusbult, Caryl E., and Bram P. Buunk. 1993. "Commitment Processes in Close Relationships: An Interdependence Analysis." *Journal of Social and Personal Relationships* 10 (2): 175–204.

Rusbult, Caryl E., Eli J. Finkel, and Madoka Kumashiro. 2009. "The Michelangelo Phenomenon." *Current Directions in Psychological Science* 18 (6): 305–9.

Sahtouris, Elisabet. 2000. *Earth Dance: Living Systems in Evolution*. Lincoln, NE: iUniverse Press.

Satir, Virginia. 1976. *Making Contact*. Berkeley, CA: Celestial Arts.

Schnarch, David Morris. 2009. *Passionate Marriage: Love, Sex, and Intimacy in Emotionally Committed Relationships*. New York: W. W. Norton & Company.

Schwartz, Jeffrey M., and Sharon Begley. 2003. *The Mind and the Brain*. New York: Springer Science & Business Media.

Seligman, Martin E. P. 2002. *Authentic Happiness: Using the New Positive Psychology to Realize Your Potential for Lasting Fulfillment*. New York: Atria Books.

Shaver, Phillip, and Mario Mikulincer. 2002. "Attachment-Related Psychodynamics." *Attachment and Human Development* 4: 133–61.

Siegel, Daniel. 2006. "An Interpersonal Neurobiology Approach to Psychotherapy: How Awareness, Mirror Neurons and Neural Plasticity Contribute to the Development of Well-Being." *Psychiatric Annals* 36: 248–58.

Siegel, Daniel J. 2010. *Mindsight: The New Science of Personal Transformation*. New York: Random House.

Siegel, Daniel J. 2012a. *The Developing Mind: How Relationships and the Brain Interact to Shape Who We Are*. New York: Guilford Press.

Siegel, Daniel J. 2012b. *Pocket Guide to Interpersonal Neurobiology: An Integrative Handbook of the Mind*. New York: W. W. Norton & Company.

Siegel, Daniel. 2007. *The Mindful Brain: Reflection and Attunement in the Cultivation of Well-Being*. New York: W. W. Norton & Company.

Stanley, Scott M. 2005. *Power of Commitment: A Guide to Active, Lifelong Love*. San Francisco: Jossey-Bass.

Stern, Daniel N. 2004. *The Present Moment in Psychotherapy and Everyday Life*. New York: W. W. Norton & Company.

Sternberg, Robert J. 1986. "A Triangular Theory of Love." *Psychological Review* 93: 119–35.

Tronick, Edward Z., and Jeffrey F. Cohn. 1989. "Infant-Mother Face-to-Face Interaction: Age and Gender Differences in Coordination and the Occurrence of Miscoordination." *Child Development*. 60: 85–92.

Tronick, Edward Z., Nadia Bruschweiler-Stern, Alexandra M. Harrison, Karlen Lyons-Ruth, Alexander C. Morgan, Jeremy P. Nahum, Louis Sander, and Daniel N. Stern. 1998. "Dyadically Expanded States of Consciousness and the Process of Therapeutic Change." *Infant Mental Health Journal* 19: 290–99.

Tsapelas, Irene, Arthur Aron, and Terri Orbuch. 2009. "Marital Boredom Now Predicts Less Satisfaction 9 Years Later." *Psychological Science* 20: 543–45.

Vogler, Christopher. 1998. *The Writer's Journey: Mythic Structure for Writers*. Studio City, CA: M. Wiese Productions.

Wilson, Timothy D., and Daniel T. Gilbert. 2000. "Miswanting: Some Problems in the Forecasting of Future Affective States." In *Feeling and Thinking: The Role of Affect in Social Cognition*, edited by Joseph Forgas. New York: Cambridge University Press.

Wilson, Timothy D., and Daniel T. Gilbert. 2005. "Affective Forecasting: Knowing What to Want." *Current Directions in Psychological Science* 14: 131–34.

Winnicott, Donald W. 1965. "Ego Distortion in Terms of the True and False Self." In *The Maturational Processes and the Facilitating Environment*. Madison, CT: International Universities Press.

Wiseman, Richard. 2013. *The As If Principle: The Radically New Approach to Changing Your Life*. New York: Free Press.

Wright, Judith, and Robert Wright. 2013. *Transformed! The Science of Spectacular Living*. New York: Turner Publishing Company.

Wright, Judith. 2006. *The Soft Addiction Solution: Break Free of the Seemingly Harmless Habits That Keep You from the Life You Want*. New York: Tarcher.

Wright, Judith. 2008. *Living a Great Life: The Theory of Evolating*. Doctorate of Education dissertation, Fielding Graduate University.

Wright, Robert, and Judith Wright. 2012. *Foundations of Lifelong Learning and Personal Transformation*. Chicago: Evolating Press.

About the Authors

Judith Wright, EdD, is a world-renowned couples and lifestyles coach, media favorite, inspirational speaker, lifestyles expert, professor, and corporate consultant. She is the award-winning coauthor of *Transformed!* and the best-selling author of *There Must Be More Than This* and *The Soft Addiction Solution*. Wright has appeared on *20/20*, *Oprah*, *Good Morning America*, and *Today*; and in over 600 print and radio interviews, including the *New York Post*, *Boston Herald*, and *San Francisco Chronicle*. Wright is cofounder of the dynamic and innovative couples program at the Wright Foundation and the Wright Graduate University for the Realization of Human Potential, where she is also professor of transformational coaching.

Bob Wright, EdD, is an internationally recognized visionary, speaker, educator, consultant, coach, professor, and best-selling author. He cofounded the Wright Graduate University for the Realization of Human Potential to teach people to develop their vision and fulfill their dreams. Coauthor of the award-winning book *Transformed!* and several other books that have sold hundreds of thousands of copies globally, Wright is recognized as a top coach by *Crain's Business* and has helped thousands of people across the country transform their careers, relationships, and lives. Wright is cofounder of the couples program at the Wright Foundation and the Wright Graduate University for the Realization of Human Potential, where he is also professor of transformational leadership.

Judith and Bob bring not only significant academic and research background to the couples skills they teach, but also real-world experience from a thriving and dynamic marriage. It's not uncommon for the Wrights to be mistaken for newlyweds—even after thirty-plus years of marriage. They model a truth-telling, no-holds-barred, intimate relationship for all the couples they lead, teach, and train.

About the Wright Foundation for the Realization of Human Potential

Our purpose is to support others to unleash their potential by consciously engaging in their own transformation and leadership, for the advancement of humanity and conscious, sustainable living on the planet.
—Wright Statement of Purpose

A 501(c)(3) nonprofit, the foundation is dedicated to bringing out the best in individuals and those they lead, coach, and serve. The foundation's mission includes training, coaching, leadership development, education, research, and thought leadership.

Training, Coaching, and Leadership Development: The foundation's innovative curriculum brings out your best and energizes your life personally and professionally. Our "**yearning-based learning**" applies both traditional and cutting-edge human emergence technologies to relationships, personal development, career, and leadership. We synthesize traditional and emerging research and training into pragmatic systems. Individuals, leaders, and coaches apply these practical, moment-by-moment skills to lead lives of contribution, meaning, and purpose.

The Wright Graduate University for the Realization of Human Potential (www.wrightgrad.edu) offers graduate certificate programs and master's and doctoral degrees in social and emotional intelligence, transformational leadership, and coaching. Students gain superior training in the kind of complex skills that today's workplace demands—leadership, strategic thinking, problem solving, communication, and team building—in an experiential learning environment where they have a sense of meaning and purpose as they embrace their own gifts and share them with the world.

Research and Thought Leadership: Thought leaders come in all shapes and sizes. From CEOs to stay-at-home moms, they represent varied religious backgrounds, ethnicities, and walks of life. What they have in common is a powerful intent to lead conscious, authentic lives filled with purpose, meaning, and contribution. These leaders are the true power behind the Wright Foundation, bringing the tools of social and emotional intelligence into education, health care, business, and society in profound and inspiring ways.

Resources

Get the most out of this book—and your relationships!

If you want to take your relationship further,
visit **www.heartofthefight.com** to find resources like these:

FREE Weekend Training for You and a Friend ($800 value/person)

Great relationships start with you. Learn to apply the skills of the *Heart of the Fight Process* for greater success in your life, relationships, career, and leadership. This weekend course is also the kickoff of our signature program where people from all walks of life learn to bring out their best. Be our guest at this powerful and inspirational training—and bring a friend!

Go to **www.heartofthefight.com/resources**.
Use the code **heartofthefightbook** to sign up for your complimentary admission.

Tools, tips, and support

Learn more about courses, coaching, tools, inspirational e-mails, and other resources to support you to bring out your best. Let us know if you'd like to have Judith or Bob, or even both, speak to your group.

Go to **www.wrightliving.com** or contact us directly at **312.645.8300** or **hello@wrightliving.com**.

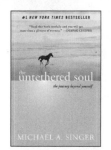
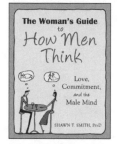
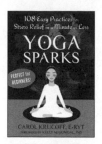

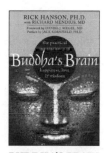